TRUE STORIES OF CRI

MW01016583

BY

FORMERLY DISTRICT ATTORNEY, NEW YORK COUNTY
1908

PREFACE

The narratives composing this book are literally true stories of crime. In a majority of the cases the author conducted the prosecutions himself, and therefore may claim to have a personal knowledge of that whereof he speaks. While no confidence has been abused, no essential facts have been omitted, distorted, or colored, and the accounts themselves, being all matters of public record, may be easily verified.

The scenes recorded here are not literature but history, and the characters who figure in them are not puppets of the imagination, but men and women who lived and schemed, laughed, sinned and suffered, and paid the price when the time came, most of them, without flinching. A few of those who read these pages may profit perhaps by their example; others may gain somewhat in their knowledge of life and human nature; but all will agree that there are books in the running brooks, even if the streams be turbid, and sermons in stones, though these be the hearts of men. If in some instances the narratives savor in treatment more of fiction than of fact, the writer must plead guilty to having fallen under the spell of the romance of his subject, and he proffers the excuse that, whereas such tales have lost nothing in accuracy, they may have gained in the truth of their final impression.

ARTHUR TRAIN.
CRIMINAL COURTS BUILDING,
NEW YORK CITY,
April 20, 1908.

I
The Woman in the Case

On a sultry August afternoon in 1903, a dapper, if somewhat anaemic, young man entered the Broadway store of Rogers, Peet & Company, in New York City, and asked to be allowed to look at a suit of clothes. Having selected one to his fancy and arranged for some alterations, he produced from his wallet a check for $280, drawn to the order of George B. Lang, and signed E. Bierstadt, and remarked to the attentive salesman:

"I haven't got quite enough cash with me to pay for these, but I have been intending to cash this check all the afternoon. Of course, you don't know me or even that my name is Lang, but if you will forward the check to the bank they will certify it, and to-morrow I will send for the suit and the balance of the money."

"Certainly, Mr. Lang," replied the salesman. "I will hold the suit and the money to await your orders."

The customer thanked him and took his departure. The check was sent to the bank, the bank certified it, then cancelled its certification and returned the check to Rogers, Peet & Company, and the store detectives, having communicated with Police Headquarters, anxiously awaited the arrival of Mr. Lang's messenger.

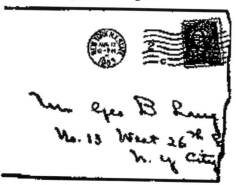

FIG. 1.—Envelope on the back of which Parker's forged order was written.

Their efforts were rewarded a couple of days later by the appearance at the store of a lad who presented a written order (Fig. 1 and Fig. 2) inscribed upon the back of an envelope bearing a cancelled stamp and addressed to Geo. B. Lang, No. 13 West Twenty-sixth Street, New York City, which read as follows:

ROGERS, PEET & Co.

Please give to bearer the clothes I purchased on Tuesday—suit—pants—S. coat, and also kindly put change in envelope in inside coat pocket. Trusting the alterations are satisfactory, and thanking you in advance for the favor and for past courtesies, I am,

Resp. yours,

GEO. B. LANG.

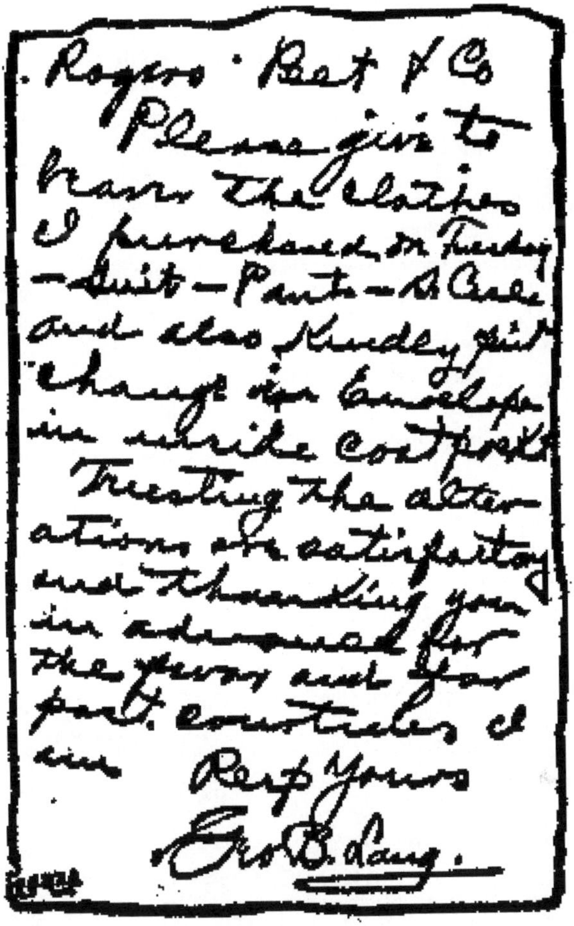

FIG. 2.—Parker's order on Rogers, Peet & Company, in the name of Lang.

The boy was immediately placed under arrest, and after proclaiming his own innocence and vociferating that he was only doing an errand for a "gent," who was waiting close by, was directed to return with his bundle as if nothing had occurred. This he did, and Mr. George B. Lang was soon in the clutches of the law.

Interrogated by his captors, the supposed Lang admitted that his real name was James Parker, that he lived at 110 West Thirty-eighth Street, and only requested that his wife be immediately notified of what had happened. At Headquarters the prisoner was identified as a gentleman who had been very actively engaged during the preceding months in passing bad checks throughout the city, his more recent operations having consisted in cashing a check on the Lincoln National Bank for $160 on July 20th, one for $290 on the same bank on July 30th, still another for $510.50 on August 4th, and one for $440.50 on the National

Shoe and Leather Bank, "to bearer," on August 8th. This last, in some inexplicable way, had been cashed at the very bank itself.

Believing that the forger had at last been caught, the precinct detectives later on, during the evening of Parker's arrest, visited no West Thirty-eighth Street, and on inquiring for "Mrs. Parker," were introduced to a young girl of attractive appearance to whom they delivered their unwelcome message. Mrs. Parker seemed overwhelmed at the news and strongly asserted her confidence in her husband's innocence of any wrong-doing. Having performed their errand the officers departed.

A certain ineradicable jealousy has always existed between the plain-clothes men of the various precincts and the sleuths attached to the Central Office, and in this instance the precinct men, having gained the credit for the arrest, it did not occur to them as necessary to communicate the knowledge of their acquaintance with Mrs. Parker to Detective Sergeants Peabody and Clark, originally assigned at Headquarters to investigate the case.

It seemed, however, to Peabody very unlikely that Parker had conducted his operations alone, and he therefore at once inquired at the Tombs what character of visitors came to see the prisoner. The gateman replied that as yet none had arrived. At that very instant a young girl stepped to the wicket and asked if she could be allowed to see Mr. James Parker. It took the detective but a moment to run across to the Criminal Courts Building and to telephone the warden to detain her temporarily and then to refuse her request. Five minutes later the girl emerged disconsolately from the Tombs and boarded a car going uptown. Peabody followed her to 110 West Thirty-eighth Street, not for an instant supposing that the girl herself could be the forger, but believing that possibly through her he might learn of other members of the gang and secure additional evidence against Parker himself.

Of course, no intelligent person to-day supposes that, outside of Sir Conan Doyle's interesting novels, detectives seek the baffling criminal by means of analyzing cigar butts, magnifying thumb marks or specializing in the various perfumes in favor among the fair sex, or by any of those complicated, brain fatiguing processes of ratiocination indulged in by our old friend, Mr. Sherlock Holmes. There are still, however, genuine detectives, and some of them are to be found upon the New York police force. The magnifying glass is not one of the ordinary tools of the professional sleuth, and if he carries a pistol at all it is because the police rules require it, while those cases may be numbered upon the fingers of two hands where his own hair and whiskers are not entirely sufficient for his purposes in the course of his professional career.

The next morning Peabody donned the most disreputable suit in his wardrobe, neglected his ordinary visit to the barber, and called at 110 West Thirty-eighth Street, being, of course, at this time entirely unaware of the fact that the girl was Parker's wife. He found her sitting in a rocking chair in a comfortable, well-furnished room, and reading a magazine. Assuming an expression of sheepish inanity he informed her that he was an old pal of "Jim's" who had been so unfortunate as to be locked up in the same cell with him at Headquarters, and that the latter was in desperate need of morphine. That Parker was an habitual user of the drug could be easily seen from the most casual inspection, but that it would prove an open sesame to the girl's confidence was, as the detective afterward testified, "a hundred-to-one shot."

"Poor Jim!" exclaimed the girl. "Couldn't you smuggle some into the Tombs for him?"

Peabody took the hint. Of course he could. It would be a hard job—those turnkeys were so suspicious. But *he* could do it for her if anybody could. He rambled on, telling his experiences with Parker in the past, how he had been in Elmira Reformatory and elsewhere with him, and gaining each moment valuable information from the girl's exclamations, questions, and expression. He soon learned that she was Parker's wife, that they were living in comparative comfort, and that she was an exceedingly clever and well-educated woman, but she said nothing during the conversation which would indicate that she knew anything of her husband's offenses or of any persons connected with them.

After a few moments the girl slipped on her coat and hat and the two started down to the Tombs, where, by prearrangement with the officials, the detective succeeded in convincing her that he had been able to send in to her husband a small hypodermic syringe (commonly called "the needles") which she had purchased at a neighboring drug store.

The apparent success of this undertaking put Mrs. Parker in excellent humor and she invited the supposed crook to breakfast with her at the Broadway Central Hotel. So far, it will be observed, Peabody had accomplished practically nothing. At breakfast the girl inquired of her companion what his particular "graft" was, to which he replied that he was an expert "second story man," and then proceeded to indulge his imagination in accounts of bold robberies in the brown stone districts and clever "tricks" in other cities, which left Mrs. Parker in no doubt but that her companion was an expert "gun" of long experience.

Then he took, as he expressed it, "another chance."

"Jim wanted me to tell you to put the gang 'wise,'" said he.

The girl looked at him sharply and contracted her brows.

"Gang?" she exclaimed. "What gang? Oh, perhaps he meant 'Dutch' and 'Sweeney.'"

Peabody bit his lip. He had had a close call.

"Don't know," he replied, "he didn't say who they were—just to put them 'wise.'"

A second time the detective had made a lucky hit, for Mrs. Parker suddenly laid aside all pretense and asked:

"Do you want to make a lot of money?"

Peabody allowed that he did.

"Do you know what they have got Jim for?" asked the girl.

"'Phoney' paper, wasn't it?"

"Yes," said Mrs. Parker, "but Jim didn't write those checks. I wrote them myself. If you want to go in with me, we can earn enough money to get Jim out and you can do a good turn for yourself besides."

The detective's blood leaped in his veins but he held himself under control as well as he could and answered indifferently.

"I guess not. I never met a woman that was very good at that sort of game."

"Oh, you don't know *me*," she persisted. "Why, I can copy anything in a few moments—really I can."

"Too dangerous," remarked Peabody. "I might get settled for ten years."

"No, you wouldn't," she continued. "It's the easiest thing in the world. All you have to do is to pick the mail out of some box on a corner. I can show you how with a copper wire and a little piece of wax—and you are sure to find among the letters somebody's check in payment of a bill. There at once you have the bank, and the signature. Then all you have to do is to write a letter to the bank asking for a new check book, saying yours is used up, and sign the name that appears on the check. If you can fool the cashier into giving your messenger a check book you can gamble pretty safely on his paying a check signed with the same name. In that way, you see, you can get all the blank checks you need and test the cashier's watchfulness at the same time. It's too easy. The only thing you have to look out for is not to overdraw the account. Still, you find so many checks in the mail that you can usually choose somebody's account that will stand the strain. Do you know, I have made *hundreds* of checks and the banks have certified every single one!"

Peabody laughed good naturedly. Things were looking up a bit.

"What do you think I am, anyhow?" he asked. "I must look like a 'come-on.'"

"I'm giving it to you straight," she said simply. "After you have made out a good fat check, then you go to a store, buy something, tell them to forward the check to the bank for certification, and that you'll send for the goods and the change the next day. The bank always certifies the check, and you get the money."

"Not always," said Peabody with a grin.

"No, not always," acquiesced Mrs. Parker. "But Jim and I have been averaging over a hundred dollars a day for months."

"Good graft, all right," assented the detective. "But how does the one who lays down the check identify himself? For instance, suppose I go into Tiffany's and pick out a diamond, and say I'm Mr. John Smith, of 100 West One Hundredth Street, and the floorwalker says, 'Sorry, Mr. Smith, but we don't know you,' what then?"

"Just flash a few letters on him," said the girl. "Letters and envelopes."

"Where do you get 'em?" asked Peabody.

"Just write them, silly, and send them to yourself through the mail."

"That's all right," retorted the "second story man." "But how can I mail myself a letter to 100 West One Hundredth Street *when I don't live there?*"

Mrs. Parker smiled in a superior manner.

"I'm glad I can put you wise to a new game, I invented it myself. You want letters of identification? In different names and addresses on different days? Very good. Buy a bundle of stamped envelopes and write your own name and address on them *in pencil*. When they arrive rub off the pencil address. Then if you want to be John Smith of 100 West One Hundredth Street, or anybody else, just address the cancelled envelope *in ink*."

"Mabel," said Peabody with admiration, "you've got the 'gray matter' all right. You can have *me*, if you can deliver the rest of the goods."

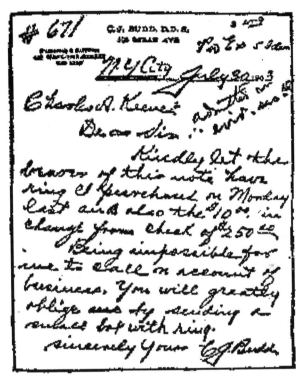

FIG.3.—A letter-head frill of Mabel Parker's.

"There's still another little frill," she continued, pleased at his compliment, "if you want to do the thing in style. Maybe you will find a letter or bill head in the mail at the same time that you get your sample check. If you do, you can have it copied and write your request for the check book and your order for the goods on paper printed exactly like it. That gives a sort of final touch, you know. I remember we did that with a dentist named Budd, at 137 West Twenty-second Street." (Fig. 3.)

"You've got all the rest whipped to a standstill," cried Peabody.

"Well, just come over to the room and I'll show you something worth while," exclaimed the girl, getting up and paying their bill.

"Now," said she, when they were safely at no West Thirty-eighth Street, and she had closed the door of the room and drawn Peabody to a desk in the bay window. "Here's my regular handwriting."

She pulled towards her a pad which lay open upon the desk and wrote in a fair, round hand:

"Mrs. James D. Singley." (Fig. 4.)

"This," she continued, changing her slant and dashing off a queer feminine scrawl, "is the signature we fooled the Lincoln National Bank with—Miss Kauser's, you know. And this," she added a moment later, adopting a stiff, shaky, hump-backed orthography, "is the signature that got poor Jim into all this trouble," and she inscribed twice upon the paper the name "E. Bierstadt." "Poor Jim!" she added to herself.

"By George, Mabel," remarked the detective, "you're a wonder! See if you can copy *my* name." And Peabody wrote the assumed name of William Hickey, first with a stub and then with a fine point, both of which signatures she copied like a flash, in each case, however, being guilty of the lapse of spelling the word Willia*m* "Willia*n*."

The pad now contained more than enough evidence to convict twenty women, and Peabody, with the remark, "You don't want to leave this kind of thing lying around, Mabel," pretended to tear the page up, but substituted a blank sheet in its place and smuggled the precious bit of paper into his pocket.

"Yes, I'll go into business with you,—sure I will!" said Peabody.

"And we'll get enough money to set Jim free!" exclaimed the girl.

They were now fast friends, and it was agreed that "Hickey" should go and make himself presentable, after which they would dine at some restaurant and then sample a convenient mail box. Meantime Peabody telephoned to Headquarters, and when the two set out for dinner at six o'clock the supposed "Hickey" was stopped on Broadway by Detective Sergeant Clark.

"What are you doing here in New York?" demanded Clark. "Didn't I give you six hours to fly the coop? And who's this woman?"

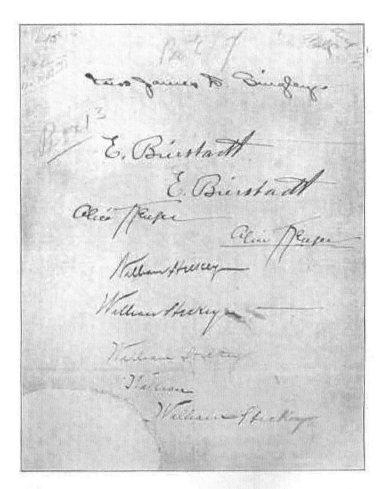

Fig. 4—The upper signature is an example of Mabel Parker's regular penmanship; the next two are forgeries from memory; and the last is a dashing imitation of her companion's handwriting.

"I was going, Clark, honest I was," whined "Hickey," "and this lady's all right—she hasn't done a thing."

"Well, I guess I'll have to lock you up at Headquarters for the night," said Clark roughly. "The girl can go."

"Oh, Mr. Clark, do come and have dinner with us first!" exclaimed Mrs. Parker. "Mr. Hickey has been very good to me, and he hasn't had anything to eat for ever so long."

"Don't care if I do," said Clark. "I guess I can put up with the company if the board is good."

The three entered the Raleigh Hotel and ordered a substantial meal. With the arrival of dessert, however, the girl became uneasy, and apparently fearing arrest herself, slipped a roll of bills under the table to "Hickey" and whispered to him to keep it for her. The detective, thinking that the farce had gone far enough, threw the money on the table and asked Clark to count it, at the same tune telling Mrs. Parker that she was in custody. The girl turned white, uttered a little scream, and then, regaining her self-possession, remarked as nonchalently as you please:

"Well, clever as you think you are, you have destroyed the only evidence against me—my handwriting."

"Not much," remarked Peabody, producing the sheet of paper.

The girl saw that the game was up and made a mock bow to the two detectives.

"I take off my hat to the New York police," said she.

At this time, apparently, no thought of denying her guilt had entered her mind, and at the station house she talked freely to the sergeant, the matron and the various newspaper men who were present, even drawing pictures of herself upon loose sheets of paper and signing her name, apparently rather enjoying the notoriety which her arrest had occasioned. A thorough search of her apartment was now made with the result that several sheets of paper were found there bearing what were evidently practice signatures of the name of Alice Kauser. (Fig. 5.) Evidence was also obtained showing that, on the day following her husband's arrest, she had destroyed large quantities of blank check books and blank checks.

Upon the trial of Mrs. Parker the hand-writing experts testified that the Bierstadt and Kauser signatures were so perfect that it would be difficult to state that they were not originals. The Parker woman was what is sometimes known as a "free hand" forger; she never traced anything, and as her forgeries were written by a muscular imitation of the pen movement of the writer of the genuine signature they were almost impossible of detection. When Albert T. Patrick forged the signature of old Mr. Rice to the spurious will of 1900 and to the checks for $25,000, $65,000 and $135,000 upon Swenson's bank and the Fifth Avenue Trust Co., the forgeries were easily detected from the fact that as Patrick had *traced* them they were *all almost exactly alike and practically could be superimposed one upon another, line for line, dot for dot.*[1]

[1] See *Infra*, p. 304.

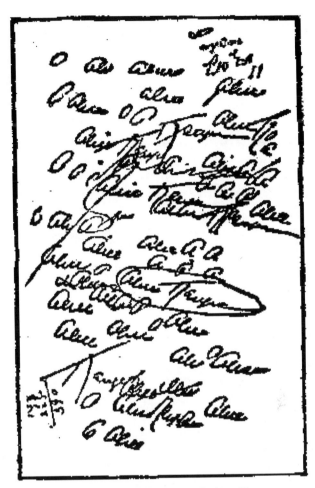

FIG. 5.—Practice signatures of the name of Alice Kauser.

Mabel Parker's early history is shrouded in a certain amount of obscurity, but there is reason to believe that she was the offspring of respectable laboring people who turned her over, while she was still an infant, to a Mr. and Mrs. Prentice, instructors in physical culture in the public schools, first of St. Louis and later of St. Paul, Minnesota. As a child, and afterwards as a young girl, she exhibited great precocity and a considerable amount of real ability in drawing and in English composition, but her very cleverness and versatility were the means of her becoming much more sophisticated than most young women of her age, with the result that while still in her teens she gave her adopted parents ground for considerable uneasiness. Accordingly they decided to place her for the next few years in a convent near New York. By this time she had attained a high degree of proficiency in writing short stories and miscellaneous articles, which she illustrated herself, for the papers and inferior magazines. Convent life proved very dull for this young lady, and accordingly one dark evening, she made her exit from the cloister by means of a conveniently located window.

Waiting for her in the grounds below was James Parker, twenty-seven years old, already of a large criminal experience, although never yet convicted of crime. The two made their way to New York, were married, and the girl entered upon her career. Her husband, whose real name was James D. Singley, was a professional Tenderloin crook, ready to turn his hand to any sort of cheap crime to satisfy his appetites and support life; the money easily secured was easily spent, and Singley, at the time of his marriage, was addicted to most of the vices common to the habitués of the under world. His worst enemy was the morphine habit and from her husband Mrs. Singley speedily learned the use of the drug. At this time Mabel Prentice-Parker-Singley was about five feet two inches in height, weighing not more than 105 or 110 pounds, slender to girlishness and showing no maturity save in her face, which, with its high color, brilliant blue eyes, and her yellow hair, often led those who glanced at her casually to think her good looking. Further inspection, however, revealed a fox-like expression, an irregularity in the position of the eyes, a hardness in the lines of the mouth and a flatness of the nose which belied the first impression. This was particularly true when, after being deprived of morphine in the Tombs, her ordinary high color gave way at her second trial to a waxy paleness of complexion. But the story of her career in the Tenderloin would prove neither profitable nor attractive.

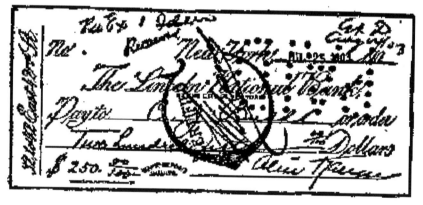

FIG. 6.—The check on which the indictment for forgery was brought.

The subsequent history of the Parker case is a startling example of the credulity of the ordinary jury. The evidence secured was absolutely conclusive, but unfortunately juries are generally unwilling to take the uncorroborated word of a policeman against that of a defendant—particularly if the defendant be a young and pretty woman. Here at the very outset was a complete confession on the part of Mrs. Parker, supplemented by illustrations from her own pen of what she could do. Comparison showed that the signatures she had written without a model upon the Peabody sheet were identical with those upon the forged checks (Fig. 6) and with Mr. Bierstadt's and Miss Kauser's handwriting. When Mrs. Parker's case, therefore, came on for pleading, her counsel, probably because they could think of nothing else to do, entered a plea of *insanity*. It was also intimated that the young woman would probably plead guilty, and the case was therefore placed upon the calendar and moved for trial without much preparation on the part of the prosecution. Instead of this young person confessing her guilt, however, she amused herself by ogling the jury and drawing pictures of the Court, the District Attorney and the various witnesses.

Probably no more extraordinary scene was ever beheld in a court of law than that exhibited by Part II of the General Sessions upon Mabel Parker's first trial for forgery. Attired in a sky blue dress and picture hat, with new white gloves, she sat jauntily by the side of her counsel throughout the proceedings toying with her pen and pencil and in the very presence of the jury copying handwriting which was given her for that purpose by various members of the yellow press who crowded close behind the rail. From time to time she would dash off an aphorism or a paragraph in regard to the trial which she handed to a reporter. If satisfactory this was elaborated and sometimes even illustrated by her for the evening edition of his paper.

The Assistant District Attorney complained that this was clearly a contempt of court, particularly as the defendant had drawn a picture not only of himself, but of the presiding justice and a witness, which had appeared in one of the evening papers. The Court, however, did not see that anything could be done about it and the girl openly continued her literary and artistic recreation. The Court itself was not a little amused at the actions of the defendant, and when Detective Peabody was called to the stand the general hilarity had reached such a pitch that he was unable to give his testimony without smiling. The natural result, therefore, at the first trial, was that the detective succeeded in giving the unqualified impression that he was drawing the long bow in a most preposterous fashion.

At the conclusion of the People's case the evidence that Mrs. Parker had forged the checks amounted simply to this: That an officer who was greatly interested in her conviction had sworn to a most astonishing series of facts from which the jury must infer that this exceedingly astute young person had not only been entirely and completely deceived by a detective, but also that at almost their first meeting she had confessed to him in detail the history of her crimes. Practically the only other evidence tending to corroborate his story were a few admissions of a similar character made by her to newspaper men, matrons and officers at the police station. Unless the jury were to believe that Mrs. Parker had actually written the signatures on "the Peabody sheet" there was no evidence that she was the actual forger; hence upon Peabody's word alone depended the verdict of the jury. The trouble with the case was that it was *too* strong, *too* good, to be entirely credible, and had there been no defense it is exceedingly probable that the trial would have resulted in an acquittal, since the prosecution had elected to go to the jury upon the question of whether or not the defendant had actually signed the checks herself.

Mrs. Parker, however, had withdrawn her plea of insanity and determined to put in a defense, which proved in its turn to be even more extraordinary than the case against her. This, in brief, was to the effect that she had known Peabody to be a police officer all along, but that it had occurred to her that if she could deceive him into believing that it was she *herself* who had committed the forgeries her husband might get off, and that later she might in turn establish her own innocence. She had therefore hastily scratched her name on the top of a sheet already containing her husband's handwriting and had told Peabody that the signatures had been written by herself. That the sheet had been written in the officer's presence she declared to be a pure invention on his part to secure her conviction. She told her extremely illogical story with a certain winsome naïveté which carried an air of semi-probability with it. From her deportment on the stand one would have taken her for a boarding school miss who in some inconsequent fashion had got mixed up in a frolic for which no really logical explanation could be given.

Then the door in the back of the court room opened and James Parker was led to the bar, where in the presence of the jury he pleaded guilty to the forgery of the very signature for which his wife was standing trial. (Kauser check, Fig. 6.) He was then sworn as a witness, took the stand and testified that *he* had written all the forged signatures to the checks, including the signatures upon "the Peabody sheet."

The District Attorney found himself in an embarrassing position. If Parker was the forger, why not challenge him to write the forged signatures upon the witness stand and thus to prove his alleged capacity for so doing? The obvious objection to this was that Parker, in anticipation of this test, had probably been practicing the signature in the Tombs for months. On the other hand if the District Attorney did not challenge him to write the signatures, the defense would argue that he was afraid to do so, and that as Parker had sworn himself to be the forger it was not incumbent upon the defense to prove it further—that that was a matter for cross examination.

With considerable hesitation the prosecuting attorney asked Parker to write the Kauser signature, which was the one set forth in the indictment charging the forgery, and after much backing and filling on the part of the witness, who ingeniously complained that he was in a bad nervous condition owing to lack of morphine, in consequence of which his hand trembled and he was in no condition to write forgeries, the latter took his pen and managed to make a very fair copy of the Kauser signature from memory, good enough in fact to warrant a jury in forming the conclusion that he was in fact the forger. (Fig. 7.) This closed the case.

The defense claimed that it was clear that James Parker was the forger, since he had admitted it in open court, pleaded guilty to the indictment and proved that he had the capacity. The prosecution, upon the other hand, argued that the evidence was conclusive that the defendant herself was the writer of the check. The whole thing boiled down to whether or not the jury was going to believe that Mrs. Parker had written "the Peabody sheet" in the presence of the detective, when her husband claimed that, with the exception of Mabel's signature, he had done it himself and carelessly left the paper in his desk in the room.

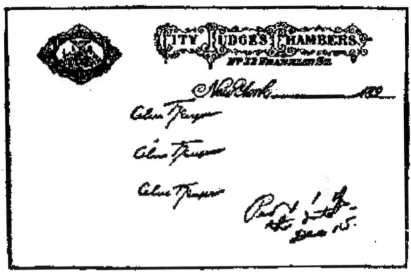

FIG. 7.—Parker's copy of the signature of Alice Kauser, made in court in an attempt to shield his wife.

The prosecuting attorney was at his wits' end for an argument to meet the fact that Parker had written a sample forgery of the Kauser signature before the very eyes of the jury. He found it at last in an offer on his own part in open court during his "summing up" to write for the jury from memory a better forgery of the Kauser signature than that written by Parker himself, and thus to show how simple a matter it was to learn to do so. He had taken up his pen and was about to give a sample of his handiwork in this respect when the defendant grasped her counsel's arm and whispered: "For God's sake, don't let him do it!" whereupon the lawyer arose and objected, saying that such evidence was improper, as the case was closed. As might have been expected under the circumstances, considering the blunders of the prosecution and the ingenuous appearance of the defendant, the trial ended in a disagreement, the jury standing eight to four for acquittal.

The District Attorney's office now took up a thorough investigation of the case, with the result that on a second prosecution Mrs. Parker was confronted with a mass of evidence which it was impossible for her to refute. A boy named Wallace Sweeney, sentenced to the Elmira Reformatory, was found to have been an active accomplice of the Parkers for several years, and he was accordingly brought down to New York, where he gave a complete history of his relations with them. His story proved beyond any doubt that Mrs. Parker was the forger of the checks in the possession of the District Attorney, and of many others beside, some of them for very large amounts. The evidence of Sweeney was of itself quite sufficient to warrant a conviction. To make assurance doubly sure, however, the District Attorney upon the second trial moved a new indictment, setting forth as the forgery a check signed "E. Bierstadt," so that when Parker took the stand, as he had done in the former trial and testified that he was the forger, he found himself unable to write this new signature, and hence his testimony went for nothing.

But even the testimony of Sweeney was that of an accomplice, requiring corroboration, while that of Peabody remained the evidence of "a mere policeman," eager to convict the defendant and "add another scalp to his official belt." With an extraordinary accumulation of evidence the case hinged on the veracity of these two men, to which was opposed the denial of the defendant and her husband. It is an interesting fact that in the final analysis of the case the jury were compelled to determine the issue by evidence entirely documentary in character. It is also an illustration of what tiny facts stamp whole masses of testimony as true or false.

On her examination Mrs. Parker had sworn among other things: (1) That she had no knowledge of the envelope, the back of which had been used by Parker for the purpose of directing Rogers, Peet & Co. to deliver the clothes and money to his messenger—and, of course, that the words "Mr. Geo. B. Lang" were not in her handwriting. This was one of the envelopes claimed by the prosecution to have been originally addressed in pencil and sent to themselves by the Parkers through the mail for this precise purpose. (2) That she had never seen the "Kauser practice sheets," and that the words "Alice Kauser," repeated hundreds of times thereon, were not in her handwriting. For some reason unknown to the District Attorney, however, she admitted having written the words "I am upstairs in the bath-room" upon a similar sheet, but claimed that at the time this was done the reverse of the paper was entirely blank.

Microscopic examination showed that among the words "Alice" and "Kauser" on the practice sheets some one had written a capital "M." One of the legs of the "M" crossed and was superimposed upon a letter in the word "Alice." Hence, whoever wrote the "M" knew what was on the practice sheet. An enlargement of this "M" and a comparison of it with the "M" in the defendant's signature to her formal examination in the police court, with the "M" in "*Mr.*" in the address on the envelope and with that in the "Mrs." on the "Peabody sheet," rendered it obvious that they were all written by one and the same hand. Therefore it was clear that the defendant was familiar with the contents of the practice sheets (Fig. 8.), even if she had not written them herself and had not told the truth in this regard.

Moreover, it was fairly easy to see that the same hand that had written the words "I am upstairs in the bath-room" upon the second practice sheet had at the same time and with the same pen written the rest of the sheet. This was clearly perceptible on examining the "e's" and "a's."

A comparison of the address "Mr. Geo. B. Lang" (on Fig. 1) with the name Mrs. James D. Singley (on Fig. 4) also shows clearly that one and the same person wrote them both. And to the accuracy of all these self-evident propositions a leading handwriting expert in New York added his unqualified opinion.

Thus, but for a little carelessness in failing to destroy odd scraps of paper and to disguise her penmanship which it seemed to her quite unnecessary to do, as in the address of the "Lang" envelope, Mrs. Parker might well have gone free after all.

It is impossible to describe all the varied dramatic features of this interesting case. No one who was present is likely to forget the impression made by the defendant at her second trial, when in defiance of overwhelming proof she still struggled to vindicate herself.

Her counsel contended throughout the trial that she was a hitherto innocent young woman led astray and started upon a criminal career by a rascally husband, whom she still loved devotedly and for whose sake she had prepared to confess herself a criminal. That James Parker introduced his wife to a life of crime there can be no doubt, but that she had a natural predilection for it must be equally obvious. It is probably true that Mabel Parker's affection for her convict husband was unfeigned and deep. The natural repugnance of the American jury for convicting a woman was shown when in spite of the overwhelming proof upon the Parker woman's second trial the jury remained out eight hours and then found her guilty of "uttering only," with a strong recommendation for mercy. She was sentenced to the Bedford Reformatory.

Fig. 8—One of the loose sheets upon which Mabel Parker illustrated her methods and her skill as a penman to the supposed ex-convict "Hickey."

II
Five Hundred Million Dollars

This story, which ends in New York, begins in the Department of the Gironde at the town of Monségur, seventy-five kilometers from Bordeaux, in the little vineyard of Monsieur Emile Lapierre—"landowner." In 1901 Lapierre was a happy and contented man, making a good living out of his modest farm. To-day he is—well, if you understand the language of the Gironde, he will tell you with a shrug of his broad shoulders that he might have been a Monte Cristo had not *le bon Dieu* willed it otherwise. For did he not almost have five hundred million dollars—two and a half *milliards* of francs—in his very hands? *Hein*? But he did! Does M'sieu' have doubts? Nevertheless it is all true. *C'est trop vrai*! Is M'sieu' tired? And would he care to hear the story? There is a comfortable chair *sous le grand arbre* in front of the veranda, and Madame will give M'sieu' a glass of wine from the presses, across the road. Yes, it *is* good wine, but there is little profit in it, when one thinks in *milliards*.

The landowner lights his pipe and seats himself cross-legged against the trunk of the big chestnut. Back of the house the vineyard slopes away toward the distant woods in straight, green, trellised alleys. A dim haze hangs over the landscape sleeping so quietly in the midsummer afternoon. Down the road comes heavily, creaking and swaying, a wain loaded with a huge tower of empty casks and drawn by two oxen, their heads swinging to the dust. Yes, it is hard to *comprendre* twenty-five hundred million francs.

It was this way. Madame Lapierre was a Tessier of Bordeaux—an ancient *bourgeois* family, and very proud indeed of being *bourgeois*. You can see her passing and repassing the window if you watch carefully the kitchen, where she is superintending dinner. The Tessiers have always lived in Bordeaux and they are connected by marriage with everybody—from the blacksmith up to the Mayor's notary. Once a Tessier was Mayor himself. Years and years ago Madame's great-uncle Jean had emigrated to America, and from time to time vague rumors of the wealth he had achieved in the new country reached the ears of his relatives—but no direct word ever came.

Then one hot day—like this—appeared M. le Général. He came walking down the road in the dust from the *gare*, in his tall silk hat and frock coat and gold-headed cane, and stopped before the house to ask if one of the descendants of a certain Jean Tessier did not live hereabouts. He was fat and red-faced, and he perspired, but—*Dieu!*—he was *distingué*, and he had an order in his buttonhole. Madame Lapierre, who came out to answer his question, knew at once that he was an aristocrat.

Ah! was she herself the grandniece of Jean Tessier? Then, Heaven be thanked! the General's toilsome journey was ended. He had much to tell them—when he should be rested. He removed the silk hat and mopped his shining forehead. He must introduce himself that he might have credit with Madame, else she might hardly listen to his story, for there had never been a tale like it before since the world was. Let him present himself—M. le Général Pedro Suarez de Moreno, Count de Tinoco and Marquis de la d'Essa. Although one was fatigued it refreshed one to be the bearer of good news, and such was his mission. Let Madame prepare herself to hear. Yes, it would be proper for her to call M'sieu', her husband, that he might participate.

Over a draft of this same vintage M. le Général imparted to them the secret. Lapierre laughs and shrugs his shoulders as he recalls the scene—the apoplectic General, with the glass of wine in one hand, waving the other grandiloquently as he described the wealth about to descend upon them.

Yes, the General must begin at the beginning, for it was a long story. First, as to himself and how he came to know of the affair. It had been on his return from the Philippines after the surrender of Manila, where he had been in command of the armies of Spain, that he had paused for repose in New York and had first learned of the Tessier inheritance. The precise manner of his discovery was left somewhat indefinite, but the Lapierres were not particular. So many distinguished persons had played a part in the drama that the recital left but a vague impression as to individuals. A certain Madame Luchia, widow of one Roquefailaire, whom he had accidentally met, had apparently been the instrument of Providence in disclosing the history of Jean Tessier to the General. She herself had been wronged by the villains and knew all the secrets of the conspirators. But she had waited for a suitable opportunity to speak. Jean Tessier had died possessed of properties which to-day, seventy years after, were worth in the neighborhood of five hundred million dollars! The General paused for the effect, solemnly nodding his head at his astounded auditors in affirmance. Yes, it was even so!

Five hundred million dollars! No more—and no less! Then he once more took up the thread of his narrative.

Tessier's lands, originally farms, were to-day occupied by huge *magasins*, government buildings, palaces and hotels. He had been a frugal, hardworking, far-seeing man of affairs whose money had doubled itself year by year. Then had appeared one Emmeric Lespinasse, a Frenchman, also from Bordeaux, who had plotted to rob him of his estate, and the better to accomplish his purpose had entered the millionaire's employ. When Tessier died, in 1884, Lespinasse had seized his papers and the property, destroyed his will, dispersed the clerks, secretaries, "notaries" and accountants of the deceased, and quietly got rid of such persons as stood actively in his way. The great wealth thus acquired had enabled him to defy those who knew that he was not entitled to the fortune, and that the real heirs were in far-away France.

He had prospered like the bay tree. His daughter, Marie Louise, had married a distinguished English nobleman, and his sons were now the richest men in America. Yet they lived with the sword of Damocles over their heads, suspended by a single thread, and the General had the knife wherewith to cut it. Lespinasse, among other things, had caused the murder of the husband of Madame Luchia, and she was in possession of conclusive proofs which, at the proper moment, could be produced to convict him of his many crimes, or at least to oust his sons and daughter from the stolen inheritance.

It was a weird, bizarre nightmare, no more astonishing than the novels the Lapierres had read. America, they understood, was a land where the rivers were full of gold—a country of bronzed and handsome savages, of birds of paradise and ruined Aztec temples, of vast tobacco fields and plantations of thousands of acres of cotton cultivated by naked slaves, while one lay in a hammock fanned by a "*petite nègre*" and languidly sipped *eau sucrée*. The General had made it all seem very, very real. At the weak spots he had gesticulated convincingly and digressed upon his health. Then, while the narrative was fresh and he might have had to answer questions about it had he given his listeners opportunity to ask them, he had hastily told of a visit to Tunis. There he had by chance encountered Marie Louise, the daughter of Lespinasse, living with her noble husband in a "handsome Oriental palace," had been invited to dine with them and had afterward seized the occasion while "walking in the garden" with the lady to disclose the fact that he knew all, and had it in his power to ruin them as impostors. Marie Louise had been frightfully angry, but afterward her better nature had suggested the return of the inheritance, or at least a hundred millions or so, to the rightful heirs. The General had left the palace believing all would be well, and had retired to Paris to await letters and further developments, but these had never come, and he had discovered that he had been deceived. It had been merely a ruse on the part of the woman and her husband to gain time, and now every step that he took was dogged by spies in the pay of the Lespinasses, who followed him everywhere. But the right would triumph! He had sworn to run the conspiracy to earth!

Many hours were consumed in the telling of the story. The Lapierres were enchanted. More than that, they were convinced—persuaded that they were heirs to the richest inheritance in the world, which comprised most of the great American city of New York.

Persons who were going to participate in twenty-five hundred millions of francs could afford to be hospitable. M. le Général stayed to dinner. A list of the heirs living in or near Bordeaux was made out with the share of each in the inheritance carefully computed. Madame Lapierre's was only fifty million dollars—but still that was almost enough to buy up Bordeaux. And they could purchase Monségur as a country place. The General spoke of a stable of automobiles by means of which the journey from Bordeaux to the farm could be accomplished in the space of an hour.

That night the good man and his wife scarcely closed their eyes, and the next day, accompanied by the General, they visited Bordeaux and the neighboring towns and broke the news gently to the other heirs. There was M. Pettit, the veterinary at Mormand; Tessier, the blacksmith in Bordeaux; M. Pelegue and his wife, M. Rozier, M. Cazenava and his son, and others. One branch of the family lived in Brazil—the Joubin Frères and one Tessier of "Saint Bezeille." These last had to be reached by post, a most annoyingly slow means of communication—*mais que voulez-vous?*

Those were busy days in and around Bordeaux, and the General was the centre of attraction. What a splendid figure he cut in his tall silk hat and gold-headed cane! But they were all very careful to let no inkling of their good fortune leak out, for it might spoil everything—give some opportunity to the spies of the impostor Lespinasse to fabricate new chains of title or to prepare for a defense of the fortune. The little blacksmith, being addicted to white wine, was the only one who did not keep his head. But even he managed to hold his mouth sufficiently shut. A family council was held; M. le Général was given full power of attorney to act for all the heirs; and each having contributed an insignificant sum toward his necessary expenses, they waved him a tremulous good-by as he stood on the upper deck of the steamer, his silk hat in one hand and his gold-headed cane in the other.

"He will get it, if any one can!" cried the blacksmith enthusiastically.

"It is as good as ours already!" echoed Rozier.

"My friends," Madame Lapierre assured them, "a General of the armies of Spain and a Chevalier of the Order of Jiminez would die rather than fail in his mission. Besides," she added, her French blood asserting itself, "he is to get nineteen per cent. of the inheritance!"

As long as the steamer remained in sight the General waved encouragingly, his hat raised toward Heaven.

"*Mais*," says Lapierre, with another shrug as he lights his pipe, "even you would have believed him. *Vraiment*! He would have deceived the devil himself!"

Up the road the wain comes creaking back again. A crow flaps across the vineyard, laughing scornfully at good M. Lapierre, and you yourself wonder if such a thing could have been possible.

On a rainy afternoon in March, 1905, there entered the writer's office in the Criminal Courts Building, New York City, a ruddy, stoutly-built man, dressed in homespun garments, accompanied by an attractive and vivacious little woman, who, while unable to speak a single word of English, had no difficulty in making it obvious that she had a story to tell of the most vital importance. An interpreter was soon found and the names of the visitors disclosed. The lady, who did the talking for both of them, introduced herself as Madame Valoie Reddon, of Bordeaux, and her companion as M. Emile Lapierre, landowner, of Monségur, They had come, she explained, from France to take possession of the inheritance Tessier. She was a personal friend of Madame Lapierre, and as the Tessiers had exhausted all their money in paying the expenses connected with securing the fortune, she, being a well-to-do gentlewoman, had come to their assistance, and for the last few months had been financing the enterprise on a fifteen per cent. basis. If Madame Lapierre was to receive ten million dollars, then, to be sure, Madame Reddon would have one million five hundred thouand dollars; but, of course, it was not for the money, but on account of friendship, that she was aiding them. I would understand that three years had elapsed since a certain distinguished General Pedro Suarez de Moreno had disclosed to the Lapierres the fact that Madame was the heiress to the greatest estate in America. M. Lapierre solemnly nodded confirmation as the lady proceeded. It was the one subject talked about in the Gironde and Bordeaux—that is, among those who had been fortunate enough to learn anything about it. And for three years the Tessiers, their wives, their sons' wives, and their connections, had been waiting to receive the glad tidings that the conspirators had been put to rout and the rightful heirs reinstated.

It was some time before the good lady succeeded in convincing her auditor that such a ridiculous fraud as she described had actually been perpetrated. But there was M. Lapierre and there was Madame Valerie Reddon sitting in the office as living witnesses to the fact. What wonderful person could this General Moreno be, who could hypnotize a hard-headed, thrifty farmer from the Gironde and a clever little French woman from Bordeaux into believing that five hundred million dollars was waiting for them on the other side of the Atlantic! I expressed my surprise. Madame Reddon shrugged her sloping shoulders. Well, perhaps it was hard for M'sieu' to believe, but then there were the proofs, the documents, the *dossier*, and, most of all, there was the General himself. Oh' if M'sieu' could see the General in his tall silk hat and gold-headed cane!

I asked for the documents. Madame Reddon opened her bag and produced a package of nearly one hundred letters, written in a fine Spanish hand. Oh! he had been a wonderful writer, this gorgeous Count de Tinoco and Marquis de la d'Essa. She had met him herself when he had been in Bordeaux. Madame Lapierre had introduced him to her, and she had heard him talk. How beautifully he talked! The stories of his experiences as General of the armies of Spain under Don Carlos and as Brigadier-General in the Philippines were as fascinating as a romance. But it was his letters which had really led her to take a personal interest in the undertaking. With a sigh Madame Valoie untied the little blue ribbon which bound up the pitiful little history. If M'sieu' would be good enough to grant the time she would begin at the beginning. Here was his first letter written after the General's return to America:

June 25, '02.

My dear M. Lapierre:

We have had a terrible voyage. A horrible storm broke loose in mid-ocean, endangering all our lives.... The waves, like mountains, threatened every instant to swallow us all; the spectacle was terrifying. I fell from the top of the stairs 'way down into the hole (*sic*), hurting my right leg in the centre of the tibia bone. The ship's doctor, who is nothing but a stupid fool, left me helpless almost the entire day.... If ever I should have dreamt what would occur to me in this trip, not for all the gold in the world would I have embarked. But, now that I am here, I shall not retreat before any obstacle, in order to arrive at the fulfillment of my enterprise, and no matter at what cost, even at that of my life. It is necessary that I succeed—my pride demands it. Those who are in the right shall triumph, that is sure.... In the mean time, will you kindly give my regards to Madame and your son, and all of your relatives, not forgetting your good old servant. Squeezing your hand cordially, I bid you adieu.

Your devoted,

Pedro S. de Moreno.

"Can you not see the waves, and observe him falling down the hole?" asks Madame Reddon,

"Mais, voici une autre."

July 11, 1902.

M. Jean Lapierre.

My dear M. Lapierre: As soon as I could walk a little I began my research for the impostors of the inheritance Tessier. Without a doubt some person who is interested in the case has already advised them of my arrival in New York, and to take the necessary precautions to lead me astray in my researches.

Already I have discovered almost everything. I know even the house in which resided the deceased before his death. It is a house of twenty-five stories high, which resembles the Church of Saint Magdalene in Paris. To-day it is the biggest bank in New York. I have visited it from top to bottom, ascending and descending in steel elevators. This is a marvelous palace; it is worth more than five million dollars. The house itself has the numbers 100, 102, 104, 106, 108, 110, 112, 114, 116 and 118. In other words, it covers the ground of ten other houses made into one.

I have also visited six houses belonging to him, which are worth millions and are located around Central Park....

As soon as the brothers Lespinasse knew that I had arrived in New York they immediately took their departure, one for Paris to find his father, Emmeric Lespinasse, the other to the city of Tuxpan, in Mexico, to visit the properties stolen from the heirs. I have come to an understanding with the Reverend Father Van Rensselaer, Father Superior of the Jesuits, and have offered him two millions for his poor, in recompense for his aid to recover and to enter into possession of the inheritance. He takes great pains, and is my veritable guide and confidant....

I have visited Central Park, also a property of the deceased; this property alone is worth more than twenty million dollars.... I have great confidence in my success, and I am almost sure to reach the goal, if you are the heirs, for here there is a mix-up by all the devils....

The wound of my leg has much improved, the consequences which I feared have disappeared, and I expect soon my complete convalescence, but the devil has bestowed upon me a toothache, which makes me almost crazy with pain. I shall leave, nevertheless, to begin my campaign.

Will you be kind enough to give my regards to your wife and son, and to our old friend, etc., etc.

PEDRO S. DE MORENO.

"May the devil bestow upon him five hundred million toothaches!" exclaims Lapierre, for the first time showing any sign of animation.

The other letters were read in their order, interspersed with Madame Reddon's explanations of their effect upon the heirs in France. His description of the elevators of steel and of the house that covered an entire block had caused a veritable sensation. Alas! those wonders are still wonders to them, and they still, I fancy, more than half believe in them. The letters are lying before me now, astonishing emanations, totally ridiculous to a prosaic American, but calculated to convince and stimulate the imagination of a *petit bourgeois*.

The General in glowing terms paints his efforts to run down the Lespinasse conspirators. Although suffering horribly from his fractured tibia (when he fell into the "hole"), and from other dire ills, he has "not taken the slightest rest." He has been everywhere—"New Orleans, Florida, to the city of Coney Island"—to corner the villains, who "flee in all directions." The daughter, Marie Louise, through whom the General expects to secure a compromise, has left for New Orleans. "Wonderful coincidence," he writes, "they were all living quietly and I believe had no intention whatever to travel, and two days after my arrival in New York they all disappeared. The most suspicious of it all is that the banker, his wife and children had left for Coney Island for the summer and to spend their holidays, and certainly they disappeared without saying good-by to their intimate friends.... I have the whole history of Tessier's life and how he made his fortune. There is a family for the use of whom we must give at least a million, for the fortune of Tessier was not his alone. He had a companion who shared his troubles and his work. According to the will they were to inherit one from the other; the companion died, and Tessier inherited everything. I do not see the necessity of your trip to New York; that might make noise and perhaps delay my negotiations." Then follows the list of properties embraced in the inheritance:

PROPERTY AND PERSONAL ESTATE OF THE HEIRS

1 The land of Central Park ceded to the
   city of New York, of the value of $5,000,000.00

2 He had at the National Bank--United
   States Bank--deposited in gold--twenty
   to thirty million dollars. He
   never withdrew anything; on the
   contrary, he always deposited his income
   there   25,000,000.00

3 The big house on Broadway, Nos. 100
   to 118, of twenty-five stories, to-day
   the largest bank in New York   5,000,000.00

4 The house on Fifth Avenue, No. 765,
   facing Central Park, to-day one of
   the first hotels of New York--Hotel
   Savoy   8,000,000.00

5 House on Fifth Avenue, No. 767, facing
   Central Park, to-day the biggest
   and most handsomest of American
   hotels, where the greatest people and
   millionaires stop--Hotel Netherland   20,000,000.00

6 Two coal mines at Folkustung in Texas   9,000,000.00

7 A petroleum mine in Pennsylvania
   (Mexican frontier)   6,000,000.00

8 Shares of silver mine at Tuxpan,
   Mexico   10,000,000.00

9 The house at Tuxpan and its grounds,
   Mexico   15,000.00

10 The pleasure home and grounds in
   Florida (New Orleans) in the city of
   Coney Island   500,000.00

11 The house which covers all the Esquare
   Plaza (no number because it is all
   alone). It is an immense palace,
   with a park and gardens, and waters
   forming cascades and labyrinths,
   facing Central Park   12,000,000.00

12 The block of houses on Fifth and Sixth
   Avenues, facing on this same Central
   Park, which, as all these grounds belong
   to him, he had put up. They
   are a hundred houses, that is called
   here a block   30,000,000.00

13 He is the owner of two railroads and
   owns shares of others in Pennsylvania
   and Canada   40,000,000.00

14 A line of steam and sail boats--Atlantic.
   The Pennsylvania and the Tessier
   and other names   100,000,000.00

15 A dock and a quay of eight hundred
   meters on the Brooklyn River for
   his ships   130,000,000.00

16 Several values and debts owed him and
   which at his death had not been collected $40,000.00

                                 $390,555,000.00

   Which is in francs   1,952,775,000
   Plus 5 per cent   976,388

   Total in francs   1,953,751,388
"Do you blame us?" asks Madame Valoie, as I listen as politely as possible to this Arabian Nights' dream of riches.
The letters continue: The General is surrounded by enemies, of which the worst are French, and he is forced continually to change his

residence in order to escape their machinations. But all this takes money. How can he go to Tuxpan or to the city of Coney Island? "You cannot know nor imagine the expense which I have had to discover that which I have discovered. I cannot live here like a miser, for the part I represent demands much of me. Every moment I change my residence, and that costs money." He adds a little touch of detail. "I must always be dressed properly, and laundry is very dear here—a shirt costs twenty-five cents to wash, and there are other necessary expenses.... You have forgotten to tell me if you have received the album of views of New York in which I have indicated the properties of the deceased, I squeeze your hand."

"Yes, and our purses too," adds Madame Valoie. "Would M'sieu' care to see the album of the Tessier properties? Yes? M'sieu' Lapierre, kindly show the gentleman."

Lapierre unbuttons his homespun coat and produces a cheap paper-covered blank book in which are pasted small photographs and woodcuts of various well-known New York buildings. It is hard not to smile.

"M'sieu' will see," continues Madame Valoie, "that the dream had something substantial about it. When we saw these pictures in Bordeaux we were on the point of giving up in despair, but the pictures convinced us that it was all true. Moreover, just at that time the General intimated that unless he had more money he might yield to the efforts of the Lespinasse family to buy him off."

Madame Valoie points vindictively to a certain paragraph in one of the letters: "Of course they are convinced that I am not for sale, not for anything.... To my regret, my very great regret, I shall be forced to capitulate if you do not come to my aid and that quickly, for I repeat to you that my funds are all gone."

"And here is his bill," continues Madame Valoie, producing a folded document composed of countless sheets of very thin paper, bound together at the edges by strips of heavier material. This, when unfolded, stretches entirely across the room and is seen to be composed of hundreds of typewritten items, of which the following may serve as illustrations:

EXPENSES IN NEW YORK

```
July 12, Train to New Orleans  .......... $25.50
  "    16, Train to Florida        .......... $ 2.50
  "    "  Dinner on train          .......... $ 2.00
  "    17, Hotel in Florida        .......... $ 2.00
  "    18, Trip to Coney Island    .......... $  .50
  "    19, Return to Florida       .......... $  .50
  "    21, Return from Florida to New Orleans $ 2.50
  "    "  Laundry                  .......... $ 1.15
Dec.  3, Return to New York       .......... $ 6.50
  "    24, Train to Vera Cruz      .......... $57.50
Jan.  4, Trip to Tuxpan           .......... $ 2.50
```

" 5, Return to Vera Cruz .... $ 2.50
" 6, Sudden night trip to Halifax,
      Nova Scotia, via Buffalo and
      Niagara Falls $50.50
" 18, Laundry for three months .... $ 5.00
      Etc., etc.

EXTRAORDINARY EXPENSES

To Agent Pushyt John, a meerschaum and amber
    cigar-holder and pipe .... $ 7.00
Tobacco jar of shell and silver .... $ 4.00
To Indian Peter South-Go, a watch, a suit,
    and a pair of shoes $16.50
To my general agent of confidential reports
    for his daughter, a gold ring and a
    feather fan .... $ 7.00
A necktie for himself and scarf pin in
    gold and with stone for the necktie ... $ 8.60
To the letter-carrier to bring me my
    correspondence and not give it to any
    one else when I should change address . $ 4.00
Invitation to the Consul and his two
    agents in Washington hotel $12.00
Several invitations to cafés and saloons
    to the Police Agents .... $ 2.00
Invitations to old employees of Jean
    Tessier, to tear from them the
    declarations .... $ 1.50
Barber expenses $11.50
Tobacco and matches, July to December,
    three packages each week, ten cents
    each .... $ 7.80
Changing hotels to lead astray the agents
    of the impostors .... $ 9.50
        Etc., etc.

"To obtain a collossal fortune as yours will be, it is necessary to spend money unstintingly and to have lots of patience. Court proceedings will be useless, as trickery and lies are necessary to get the best of the scoundrels. It is necessary also to be a scoundrel."

"That he might well say," interpolates Lapierre. "He succeed, c'est sure."

I rapidly glanced over the remaining letters. The General seems always to be upon the verge of compelling a compromise. "I have already prepared my net and the meshes are tightly drawn so that the fish will not be able to escape.... For an office like this one needs money—money to go quickly from one place to another, prosecute the usurpers, not allow them an instant's rest. If they go to some city run after them at once, tire them with my presence and constantly harass them, and by this means compel them to hasten a compromise—"

The General is meeting with superhuman obstacles. In addition to his enemies he suffers all sorts of terrible bodily afflictions. Whenever the remittances from the Lapierres do not arrive the difficulties and diseases increase.

At last, however, after an interval of two years, things took a turn for the better. A "confidential representative" of the conspirators—one "Mr. Benedict-Smith"—arrived to make a bona fide offer of one hundred and fifty million dollars in settlement of the case. The General writes at great length as to exactly in what proportion the money should be divided among the heirs. The thing is so near a culmination that he is greatly exercised over his shabby appearance.

I am without a son and too badly dressed to go before the banker in the very likely case of his arrival here. Send me my baggage at once with the first steamer, and mark each piece "fragile." This is all. My regards to Madame Lapierre and your son. I am cordially yours, squeezing your hand.

PEDRO S. DE MORENO.

But the Lapierres and Tessiers, while not for an instant distrusting the honesty of the General, had become extremely weary of sending him money. Each heir felt that he had contributed enough toward the General's "expenses and invitations." Even the one hundred and fifty millions within easy reach did not prompt immediate response.

About the same time an extraordinary messenger arrived at the Lapierre farm, purporting to come from the Ministry of Foreign Affairs, and instructing Lapierre to repair immediately to Paris. The messenger explained that the presence of Lapierre was desired at the Ministry in connection with some investigation then in progress into the affairs of one Jean Tessier. Then the messenger departed as mysteriously as he had arrived.

Good M. Lapierre was highly excited. Here was indubitable evidence of the truth of the General's assertions. But, just as the latter had intended, perhaps, the worthy farmer jumped to the conclusion that probably the messenger from Paris had been sent by the conspirators.

"At the last moment," wrote Lapierre to Moreno, "I received from Paris a letter commanding me to go to the Ministry, and at the same time a telegram recommending that I leave at once. I shall write you from Paris all that I learn to your interest. If this letter should not reach you sealed in red wax, with small indentations made with a sewing thimble and my initials, which I always sign, it is that our correspondence is seized and read."

Events followed in rapid succession. Lapierre, the Tessiers, including the little blacksmith, became almost hysterical with excitement. A gentleman, by name "Mr. Francis Delas," called upon Lapierre and offered him twenty-five million dollars spot cash for his wife's share in the Tessier inheritance. This person also claimed that he had a power of attorney from all the other heirs, with the exception of Pettit and Rozier, and asserted that he was on the point of embarking for New York in their interest. He urged Lapierre to substitute him for Moreno. But Lapierre, now convinced that everything was as the General had claimed it to be, indignantly rejected any such proposition aimed at his old friend, and sent Mr. Francis Delas packing about his business.

"This is what my answer has been to him: 'Sir, we have already an agent with whom we can only have cause to be satisfied, so that your services are not acceptable or needed.' He left me most dissatisfied and scolding."

The sending of this confederate on the part of the wily General had precisely the effect hoped for. Lapierre and his friends were now convinced that the inheritance Tessier was a reality, and that powerful personages were not only exerting their influence to prevent the rightful heirs from obtaining their property, but had also in some way secured the cooperation of government officials. It was agreed, on all hands, that the worthy landowner, accompanied by Madame Reddon, had better proceed at once to the scene of operations and unite with the General in their common purpose. Once on the ground Lapierre could assume direction of his own campaign.

Lapierre and Madame Reddon accordingly sailed for America and arrived in New York on the fourth of December, 1904, where they were met on the dock by the General, who, freshly barbered, and with a rose in his buttonhole, invited them, as soon as they had recovered from the fatigue of landing, to make a personal inspection of their properties.

These heirs to hundreds of millions of dollars were conducted by the "Marquis de la d'Essa and Count de Tinoco" to the Battery, where he gallantly seated them in an electric surface car, and proceeded to show them the inheritance. He pointed out successively Number 100 Broadway, the "Flatiron" Building, the Fifth Avenue Hotel and the Holland House, the Waldorf-Astoria, the Vanderbilt mansion at Fifty-seventh Street and Fifth Avenue, the Hotel Savoy and the Hotel Netherland, incidentally taking a cross-town trip to the ferry station at East Twenty-third Street, and to Bellevue Hospital. A public omnibus conveyed them around Central Park—also their own. And, in spite of the cold weather, the General insisted on showing them the "Tessier mansion and estate at Fort George"—visible from the Washington Bridge—"a beautiful property in the centre of a wood." Returning, he took them to the Museum of Natural History and to the Metropolitan Museum of Art, which contained "Tessier's collections."

Having thus given them a bird's-eye view of the promised land, the General escorted them to his apartments and allowed them to see the Ark of the Covenant in the shape of a somewhat dilapidated leather trunk, which contained a paper alleged to be the will of Jean Tessier, made in Bellevue Hospital (one of his possessions), and unlawfully seized by the Lespinasse family. It was only, Moreno alleged, through the powerful influence of the Jesuits that he had been able to secure and keep a copy of this will.

Although the Marquis de la d'Essa must have known that his days were numbered, he was as gay and as entertaining as ever. Then, suddenly, the scales began to fall from Madame Reddon's eyes. The promised meeting with Marie Louise Lespinasse and her mysterious representative, "Mr. Benedict-Smith," was constantly adjourned; the "police agents," whom it had been so necessary to entertain and invite to saloons and cafés, were strangely absent, and so were the counsellors, Jesuit Fathers, bankers, and others who had crowded the General's antechambers. A slatternly Hibernian woman appeared, claiming the hero as her husband; his landlady caused him to be evicted from her premises; and his trunk containing the famous "*dossier*" was thrown into the street, where it lay until the General himself, placing it upon his princely shoulders, bore it to a fifteen-cent lodging-house.

"And now, M'sieu'," said little Madame Reddon, raising her hands and clasping them entreatingly before her, "we have come to seek vengeance upon this *misérable*! This *villain m'sieu*! He has taken our money and made fools of us. Surely you will give us justice!"

"Yes," echoed Lapierre stubbornly, "and the money was my own money, which I had made from the products of my farming."

A month later Don Pedro Suarez de Moreno, Count de Tinoco, Marquis de la d'Essa, and Brigadier-General of the Royal Armies of the Philippines and of Spain, sat at the bar of the General Sessions, twirling his mustache and uttering loud snorts of contempt while Lapierre and Madame Reddon told their story to an almost incredulous yet sympathetic jury.

But the real trial began only when he arose to take the witness chair in his own behalf. Apparently racked with pain, and laboring under the most frightful physical infirmities, the General, through an interpreter, introduced himself to the jury by all his titles, asserting that he had inherited his patents of nobility from the "Prince of Arras," from whom he was descended, and that he was in very truth "General-in-Chief of the Armies of the King of Spain, General Secretary of War, and Custodian of the Royal Seal." He admitted telling the Lapierres that they were the heirs of five hundred million dollars, but he had himself honestly believed it. When he and the rest of them had discovered their common error they had turned upon him and were now hounding him out of revenge. The courtly General was as *distingué* as ever as he addressed the hard-headed jury of tradesmen before him. As what *canaille* he must have regarded them! What a position for the "Count de Tinoco"!

Then two officers entered the courtroom bearing the famous trunk of the General between them. The top tray proved to contain thousands of railroad tickets. The prosecutor requested the defendant to explain their possession.

"Ah!" exclaimed Moreno, twirling his mustaches, "when I was General under my King Don Carlos, in the Seven Years' War of '75 and also in Catalonia in '80, I issued these tickets to wounded soldiers for their return home. At the boundaries the Spanish tickets were exchanged for French tickets." He looked as if he really meant it.

Then the prosecutor called his attention to the fact that most of them bore the date of 1891 and were printed in French—not in Spanish. The prisoner seemed greatly surprised and muttered under his breath vaguely about "plots" and "conspiracies." Then he suddenly remembered that the tickets were a "collection," made by his little son.

Beneath the tickets were found sheaves of blank orders of nobility and blank commissions in the army of Spain, bearing what appeared to be the royal seal. These the General asserted that he had the right to confer, by proxy, for his "King Don Carlos." Hundreds of other documents bearing various arms and crests lay interspersed among them. The prisoner drew himself up magnificently.

"I was the General Secretary of War of my King," said he. "When I had to give orders to the generals under me, of whom I was the chief, I had the right to put thereon the royal imprint of Don Carlos. I was given all the papers incident to the granting of orders and grades in the army, and I had the seal of the King—the seal of the Royal King."

But, unfortunately for the prisoner, the seals upon the papers turned out to be the legitimate arms of Spain and not those of Don Carlos, and as a finale he ingenuously identified the seal of the Mayor of Madrid as that of his "Royal King."

Next came a selection of letters of nobility, sealed and signed in the name of Pope Leo the Thirteenth. These, he asserted, must have been placed there by his enemies. "I am a soldier and a general of honor, and I never did any such trafficking," he cried grandly, when charged with selling bogus patents of nobility.

He explained some of his correspondence with the Lapierres and his famous bill for twelve thousand dollars by saying that when he found out that the inheritance Tessier did not exist he had conceived the idea of making a novel of the story—a "fantastic history"—to be published "in four languages simultaneously," and asserted solemnly that he had intended printing the whole sixteen feet of bill as part of the romance.

Then, to the undisguised horror of the unfortunate General, at a summons from the prosecutor an elderly French woman arose in the audience and came to the bar. The General turned first pale, then purple. He hotly denied that he had married this lady in France twenty-three years ago.

"Name of a name! He had known her! Yes—certainly! But she was no wife of his—she had been only his servant. The other lady—the Hibernian—was his only wife." But the chickens had begun to come home to roost. The pointed mustaches drooped with an unmistakable look of dejection, and as he marched back to his seat his shoulders no longer had the air of military distinction that one would expect in a general of a "Royal King." His head sank on his chest as his deserted wife took the stand against him—the wife whom, he had imagined, he would never see again.

Any one could have seen that Elizabeth de Moreno was a good woman. Her father's name, she said, was Nichaud, and she had first met the prisoner twenty-three years ago in the village of Dalk, in the Department of the Tarne, where, in 1883, he had been convicted and sentenced for stealing bed linen from the Hôtel Kassam. She had remained faithful to him in spite of his disgrace, and had visited him daily in prison, bringing him milk and tobacco. On his liberation she had married him and they had gone to live in Bordeaux. For years they had lived in comfort, and she had borne him eight children. He had never been to any war and was neither a general nor, so far as she had known, a friend of Don Carlos. She had supposed that her husband held some position in connection with the inspection of railroads, but, in 1902, it had come out that he was in the business of selling counterfeit railroad tickets, and had employed a printer named Paul Casignol to print great numbers of third-class tickets for the purpose of selling them to ignorant soldiers and artisans. Moreno had fled to America. She had then discovered that he had also made a practice of checking worthless baggage, *stealing it himself* and then presenting claims therefor against the railroad companies. She had been left without a sou, and the rascal had taken everything she had away with him, including even the locket containing the hair of her children. By the time she had finished her story Moreno's courage had deserted him, the jury without hesitation returned a verdict of guilty, and the judge then and there sentenced the prisoner to a term at hard labor in State's prison.

*   *   *   *   *

"*Mais oui*," grunts Lapierre, as the crow, with a final caw of contempt, alights in a poplar farther down the road, "I don't blame the bird for laughing at me. But, after all, there is nothing to be ashamed of. Is one to be blamed that one is fooled? *Hein*! We are all made fools of once and again, and, as I said before, he would have deceived the devil himself. But perhaps things are better as they are. Money is the root of all evil. If I had an automobile I should probably be thrown out and have my neck broken. But if M'sieu' intends to take the next train for Bordeaux it is as well that he should be starting."

III
The Lost Stradivarius

In the year 1885 Jean Bott, a native of Hesse Cassel, Germany, emigrated with his wife Matilda to this country, bringing with him a celebrated violin known as "The Duke of Cambridge Stradivarius," which he had purchased in 1873 for about three thousand thalers—a sum representing practically the savings of a lifetime. Bott had been leader of a small orchestra in Saxe Meiningen as early as 1860, and was well advanced in years before he determined to seek his fortune in America. His wife was an elderly woman and they had no offspring.

"This violin, my husband and myself made up the family—I loved it like a child," she testified at the trial.

So also did Bott, the old musician, love his instrument, and no hand but his own was ever permitted to lift it from its case or dust its darkly-glowing surface.

Whatever may have been its owner's genius, he prospered little in the new world, and, although he labored conscientiously at his profession, the year 1894 found him still giving lessons upon the violin to only half a dozen pupils, and living in two rooms at 355 West Thirty-first Street. But Bott, having the soul of a true musician, cared but little for money and was happy enough so long as he could smoke his old meerschaum pipe and draw the bow across the cherished violin held lovingly to his cheek. Then hard times came a-knocking at the door. The meagre account in the savings-bank grew smaller and smaller. The landlord, the doctor and the grocer had to be paid. One night Bott laid down his pipe and, taking his wife's wrinkled hand in his, said gently:

"Matilda, there is nothing else—we must sell our violin!"

"Even so!" she answered, turning away her face that her husband might not see the tears. "As God wills."

The next day "The Duke of Cambridge Stradivarius" was offered for sale by Victor S. Flechter, a friend of Bott's, who was a dealer in musical instruments at 23 Union Square. It so happened that Nicolini, the husband of Adelina Patti, was ambitious to own a genuine Stradivarius, and had been looking for one for a long time, and, although he was but an indifferent player, he had, in default of skill to perform, the money to buy. The matter was easily adjusted by Flechter, and Nicolini drew his check for the sum specified, which, properly certified, was tendered to Bott. But Bott had never seen a certified check and was unaccustomed to the ways of business.

"If I part with my violin I must have real money—money that I can feel—money that I can count. It was that kind of money that I paid for my violin," said he doggedly.

Nicolini, in a rage, believing himself insulted, tore the check to bits and declared the transaction at an end.

Now the price agreed upon for the violin had been forty-five hundred dollars, of which Flechter was to receive five hundred dollars as his commission, and when, through old Professor Bott's stubbornness, the sale fell through, the dealer was naturally very angry. Out of this incident grew the case against Flechter.

The old musician was accustomed to leave his treasured instrument in the lowest drawer of his bureau at the boarding-house. He always removed it before his pupils arrived and never put it back until their departure, thus insuring the secrecy of its hiding-place, and only his wife, his sister-in-law, Mollenhauer, a friend, and Klopton, a prospective purchaser, knew where it lay.

On the morning of March 31, 1894, not long after the Nicolini incident, Bott gave a single lesson to a pupil at the boarding-house, and after his midday meal set out with his wife for Hoboken to visit a friend. The violin was left in its customary place. It was dark when they returned, and after throwing off his coat and lighting the gas the old man hastened to make sure that his precious violin was safe. When he pulled out the drawer it was empty. The Stradivarius was gone, with its leather case, its two bows and its wooden box.

Half distracted the musician and his wife searched everywhere in the room, in closets, under beds, even behind the curtains, before they could bring themselves to admit that the violin had in fact disappeared. Frantically Bott called for Ellen, the servant girl. Yes, there had been a caller—a young man with dark hair and a small, dark mustache—at about five o'clock. He had waited about half an hour and then had said that he guessed he would go. She had not noticed that he took anything away with him. In his despair the old man turned to his old friend Flechter, and the next day the dealer came to express his sympathy. He urged Bott to notify the police of the theft, but the old man was prostrated with grief, and it was the wife who, with Ellen Clancy, finally accompanied Flechter to Police Headquarters. The police had no idea who had taken the old fellow's fiddle, and did not particularly care anyway. Later they cared a good deal.

Bott now began an endless and almost hopeless search for his beloved instrument, visiting every place where violins were sold, every pawnshop and second-hand store again and again until the proprietors began to think the old man must be crazy. Sometimes Flechter went with him. Once, the two travelled all the way over to New Jersey, but the scent proved to be a false one. Bott grew thinner and older week by week, almost day by day. When the professor did not feel equal to going outdoors Mrs. Bott went for him, and on these occasions often called at Flechter's store to report progress, ask his advice and secure his encouragement.

One day during one of these visits in the July following the loss of the violin Flechter handed Mrs. Bott a sheet of paper, saying:

"I have written something down here. If you have that printed and put a reward to it you will get your violin back."

The wording, partly printed and partly written in script, ran as follows:
VIOLIN LOST. $500 REWARD.

No questions asked for return of instrument taken from residence of Jean Bott March 31, 1894, 355 W. 31st St. Absolute safety and secrecy guaranteed. Victor S. Flechter, No. 21 Union Square, violin maker and dealer.

Mrs. Bott thanked him and took the notice away with her, but its publication had no result. The old professor began to fail, he no longer had an instrument upon which to teach his pupils, and those he could avail himself of seemed harsh and discordant. He had no appetite, and even found no solace in his pipe. Almost penniless they were forced to give up their lodgings and move to Hoboken. Mrs. Bott still kept up the search, but the professor could no longer tramp the streets looking for his violin. He sat silent in his room, slowly, surely, dying of a broken heart.

In course of time some one advised Mrs. Bott to lay her case before the District Attorney, and accordingly, during the summer, she visited the Criminal Courts Building and told her story to Colonel Allen, one of the assistants, who became greatly interested. The overwrought old woman had begun to suspect everybody, and even to accuse her husband's friend, Flechter, of a lack of any real interest. She thought he ought to be able to find the violin if he really made the effort. Allen began to take notice. The sleuth in him pricked up its ears. Why, sure, certainly, Flechter was the one man who knew what Bott's violin was really worth—the one man who could sell it to advantage—and he had been done out of five hundred dollars by the old musician's stupidity. Allen thought he'd take a look into the thing. Now, there lived in the same boarding-house with Allen a friend of his named Harry P. Durden, and to Durden Allen recounted the story of the lost violin and voiced his suspicions of Flechter. Durden entered enthusiastically into the case, volunteering to play the part of an amateur detective. Accordingly Durden, accompanied by a Central Office man named Baird, visited Flechter's place of business and the two represented themselves as connoisseurs in violins and anxious to procure a genuine Strad. for a certain Mr. Wright in St. Paul. Flechter expressed entire confidence in his ability to procure one, and did almost succeed in purchasing for them the so-called "Jupiter Strad."

All this took time, and at last, on April 28th, 1895, poor old Bott died in his boarding-house in Hoboken. After the funeral the widow settled up her affairs, changing her boarding place temporarily, and, having no ties in this country, determined to return to end her days in the Fatherland. On May 21st she wrote to Flechter, who had lost all track of her, that her husband had died, that she had moved to 306 River Street, Hoboken, and that she thought seriously of going back to Germany. Two days later Flechter wrote the following letter to the Central Office man, who had given his name as Southan, an employe of the alleged Mr. Wright:

MR. SOUTHAN, care of H. P. Durden.

Dear Sir: Write to inform you that I have a genuine Strad. to offer you and would like to see you at your earliest convenience.

Very respectfully yours,

VICTOR S. FLECHTER.

When Allen saw this letter it seemed to him absolutely to confirm his suspicions. Now that the only person in the world who had been authoritatively able to identify the "Duke of Cambridge" Stradivarius was dead, Flechter was offering one for sale.

Then occurred the strangest thing of all. On May 28th, five days after Flechter's letter to Southan, Mrs. Bott received the following extraordinary epistle. Like the notice given her by Flechter in his office, it was partly written in printed capitals and partly in script.

May 28, 1895.

To MRS. BOTT, 306 River Street, Hoboken, N. J.

Dear Madam: I wish to inform you that the violin taken from your house some time ago will be returned if you are willing to abide by agreements that will be made between you and I later on. It was my intention first to dispose of it, but on account of its great value and the danger it would place me in by offering for sale being a violin maker and dealer and not being able to sell with safety for such a large sum of money I concluded to wait. I have now thought the matter over and come to the conclusion that a little money is better than none and if you are anxious for the return of the violin and willing to pay a sum of money, small compared with the value of the violin, I think we can make a deal. You can put a personal in the New York Sun saying I am willing to give a sum of money for the return of the violin. No questions asked. Mrs. J. Bott. When I see your personal in the Sun I will let you know how the exchange can be made. CAVE DWELLER.

This letter appeared to be written in a somewhat similar hand to that which penned the offer of the reward, which, according to Mrs. Bott, was Flechter's. By this time the widow and Allen, were in close communication. The "Cave Dweller" letter, could it be shown to be in Flechter's penmanship, seemed to fix the crime on the violin dealer.

Flechter's store is two flights up and looks out into Union Square. Before the window hangs a large gilded fiddle and the walls are decorated with pictures of famous musicians. In the rear is a safe where the more valuable instruments are kept; in the front sits Flechter himself, a stoutish man of middle height, with white hair and mustache. But on June 23, 1895, Flechter was out when Durden and Baird called, and only his clerk and office-boy were on hand. Durden wished, he said, to see the genuine Strad. about which Mr. Flechter had written him. The boy went to the safe and brought back a violin in a red silk bag. Inside was inscribed:

"Antonius Stradivarius Cremonis fecit Anno Domini 1725."

The figures 17 were printed and the 25 written in ink. Durden examined it for some fifteen minutes and noted certain markings upon it.

On June 26th they called again, found Flechter in and asked to see the violin. This time the dealer took it himself from the safe, and, at their request, carried it to 22 Gramercy Park, where Durden said he desired some experts to pass upon its genuineness. On the way over Flechter guaranteed it to be a genuine Strad., and said it belonged to a retired merchant named Rossman, who would expect to get four thousand dollars for it. He himself would want five hundred dollars, and Durden should have five hundred dollars, so that they must not take less than five thousand dollars.

Once at Allen's boarding-house Flechter played upon the violin for Durden and the supposed Southan, and then the former asked to be allowed to take the instrument to a rear room and show it to a friend. Here Mrs. Bott, positively identified the violin as that of her husband, clasping it to her bosom like a long-lost child. This was enough for Durden, who gave the instrument back to Flechter and caused his arrest as he was passing out of the front gate. The insulted dealer stormed and raged, but the Car of Juggernaut had started upon its course, and that night Flechter was lodged in the city prison. Next morning he was brought before Magistrate Flammer in the Jefferson Market Police Court and the violin was taken out of its case, which the police had sealed. At this, the first hearing in this extraordinary case, Mrs. Bott, of course, identified the violin positively as "The Duke of Cambridge," and several other persons testified that, in substance, it was Bott's celebrated violin. But for the defendant a number of violin makers swore that it was not the Bott violin at all, and more—that it was not even a Stradivarius. One of them, John J. Eller, to whom it will be necessary to revert later, made oath that the violin was *his*, stolen from him and brought to Flechter by the thief. On this testimony the magistrate naturally decided that the identity of the instrument had not been established and ordered that Flechter be discharged and the violin returned to him.

Ordinarily that would have been the end of the case, but Allen had his own private views as to the guilt of the dealer and on August 28th the Grand Jury filed an indictment against Flechter accusing him of feloniously receiving stolen property—the violin—knowing it to have been stolen. Great was Flechter's anger and chagrin, but he promptly gave bail and employed the ablest counsel he could afford.

Now began the second act of this tragedy of errors. The case was called for trial with the People's interests in the hands of James W. Osborne, just advancing into the limelight as a resourceful and relentless prosecutor. I say the *People's* case but perhaps *Allen's* case would be a more fitting title. For the defense Arthur W. Palmer held the fort, directing his fire upon Osborne and losing no advantage inadvertently given him. The noise of the conflict filled the court house and drowned the uproar on Broadway. Nightly and each morning the daily press gave columns to the proceedings. Every time the judge coughed the important fact was given due prominence. And every gibe of counsel carried behind it its insignia of recognition—"[*Laughter*]" It was one of those first great battles in which the professional value of compressed air as an explosive force and small pica type as projectiles was demonstrated. It was a combat of wind and lead—an endurance contest during which the jury slept fitfully for three long weeks.

Two things, the prosecution claimed, proved Flechter's guilt: first, the fact that the violin found in his possession was "The Duke of Cambridge"; second, that the "Cave-Dweller" letter was in the same handwriting as Flechter's notice of reward.

Of course the latter proposition carried with it the necessity of proving in the first place that the notice itself was in Flechter's penmanship. Flechter through his counsel said it wasn't, and that he had never told Mrs Bott that it was. He claimed that his brother-in-law, John D. Abraham, had written it. Mrs. Bott, he alleged, was an old lady and was mistaken in her testimony when she swore that he had said, "I have written down something." He had not said so. Mr. Abraham corroborated him. He had written it himself sitting in an armchair, all but the words "355 West Thirty-first Street," which had been put in by a certain Mr. Jopling who had been present. Mr. Jopling swore that that was so, too.

But, on cross-examination, it developed that Mr. Abraham had been practicing making copies of the notice at the suggestion of the lawyer for the defense, and, when Mr. Jopling took the stand, he was called upon to explain an affidavit made by him for Assistant District Attorney Allen, in which he affirmed that he did not know *who* wrote the words "355 West Thirty-first Street." His explanation did not explain, and, anyhow, there did not seem to be any particular reason why Abraham and Jopling should have written Flechter's notice for him. Besides, even if Flechter did *not* write it and Abraham *did*, it would still remain almost as bad for Flechter if it was shown that "Cave Dweller" was his own brother-in-law.

But Mrs. Bott was a woman who appealed strongly to a jury's sympathies, and she was clear that Flechter had said that he had written the notice. Moreover, she recalled that the date had first been written *May* and that Flechter had erased it and inserted *March* in its place. A microscopic examination revealed the fact that such an erasure had been made. When the smoke cleared the credibility of the defense appeared badly damaged. But the precise point was of little importance, after all. The great question was: the identity of 'CAVE DWELLER.' On this point a number of witnesses testified from a general knowledge of Flechter's handwriting that the "Cave Dweller" letter was his, and three well-known handwriting "experts" (Dr. Persifor Frazer, Mr. Daniel T. Ames and Mr. David Carvalho) swore that, in their opinion, the same hand had written it that had penned the notice.

It is not unlikely that Flechter's fear of a conviction led him to invite testimony in his behalf which would not bear the test of careful scrutiny. Many an innocent man has paid the penalty for uncommitted crime because he has sought to bolster up his defense with doubtful evidence without the incubus of which he would have been acquitted.

Naturally the chief point against Flechter, if it could be established, was his actual possession of the Bott Stradivarius when he was arrested. Upon this proposition Mrs. Bott was absolutely positive beyond the possibility of error. So were eight other witnesses for the prosecution. Then the defense produced a violin alleged to be the same one exhibited in the police court and brought by Flechter to Durden's house, and asked Mrs. Bott and her witnesses what they thought of it. Mrs. Bott could not identify it, but she swore no less positively that it was an entirely *different* violin from the one which she had seen before the magistrate. Then Osborne hurled his bomb over his enemy's parapet and cried loudly that a monstrous wicked fraud had been perpetrated to thwart Justice—that the defense had "faked" another violin and were now trying to foist the bogus thing in evidence to deceive the Court. *Ten witnesses* for the prosecution now swore that the violin so produced was *not* the one which Flechter had tried to sell Durden. Of course it would have been comparatively easy to "fake" a violin, just as Osborne claimed, and the case sheds some light upon the possibilities of the "old violin" industry.

The star witness for the prosecution to prove that the instrument produced in the police court *was* the Bott violin was August M.

Gemunder, and his testimony upon the trial before Recorder Goff is worthy of careful examination, since the jury considered it of great importance in reaching a verdict, even requesting that it should be re-read to them some hours after retiring to deliberate. Gemunder testified, in substance, that he belonged to a family which had been making violins for three generations and had himself been making them for twenty years, that he was familiar with Bott's Stradivarius, having seen it three times, and that he firmly believed a large part of the violin produced before the magistrate *was* the missing Bott—certainly the back and scroll. Moreover, he was able to describe the markings of the Bott violin even to the label inside it. It should be mentioned, however, that in the magistrate's court he had been called only to *describe* the Bott violin and not to *identify* the one produced as the Bott itself. He further swore that the violin now offered by the defense on the trial was *not* the one in evidence before the magistrate, but was one which he had sold some years before to one Charles Palm.

The defense, on the other hand, called among its witnesses John P. Frederick, a violin maker, who testified that he was familiar with the Bott Strad. and had seen it in 1873 at Bott's house, Grenecher Castle, in Germany; that he had repaired it in this country in 1885; that the instrument in court was not a Strad. nor even a good imitation of one, and, of course, was not the "Duke of Cambridge," but that it *was* the identical instrument produced before the magistrate, and one which he recognized as having been sent him for repair by Charles Palm in 1885.

Thus both sides agreed that the fiddle now offered in evidence was a bogus Strad. once belonging to a man named Palm, the only element of conflict being as to whether or not the violin which Flechter had offered for sale was the Palm instrument, or, in fact, Bott's famous "Duke of Cambridge."

All this technical testimony about violins and violin structure naturally bored the jury almost to extinction, and even the bitter personal encounters of counsel did not serve to relieve the dreariness of the trial. One oasis of humor in this desert of dry evidence gave them passing refreshment, when a picturesque witness for the defense, an instrument maker named Franz Bruckner, from South Germany, having been asked if the violin shown him was a Strad., replied, with a grunt of disgust: "Ach Himmel, nein!" Being then invited to describe all the characteristics of genuine Stradivarius workmanship, he tore his hair and, with an expression of utter hopelessness upon his wrinkled face, exclaimed despairingly to the interpreter:

"Doctor, if I gave you lessons in this every day for three weeks you would know no more than you do now!"—an answer which was probably true, and equally so of the jury who were shouldered with the almost impossible task of determining from this mass of conflicting opinion just where the truth really lay.

The chief witness for the defense was John J. Eller, who testified that he had been a musician for thirty years and a collector of violins; that the violin in court was the same one produced before the magistrate, and was not Bott's, but *his own*; that he had first seen it in the possession of Charles Palm in 1886 in his house in Eighth Street and St. Mark's Place, New York City, had borrowed it from Palm and played on it for two months in Seabright, and had finally purchased it from Palm in 1891, and continued to play in concerts upon it, until having been loaned by him to a music teacher named Perotti, in Twenty-third Street, it was stolen by the latter and sold to Flechter.

It appeared that Eller had at once brought suit against Flechter for the possession of the instrument, which suit, he asserted, he was still pressing in the courts, and he now declared that the violin was in exactly the same condition in every respect as when produced in the police court, although it had been changed in some respects since it had been stolen. It had originally been made of baked wood by one Dedier Nicholas (an instrument maker of the first half of the nineteenth century), and stamped with the maker's name, but this inscription was now covered by a Stradivarius label. Eller scornfully pointed out that no Strad. had ever been made of baked wood, and showed the jury certain pegs used by no other maker than Nicholas, and certain marks worn upon the instrument by his, the witness', own playing. He also exhibited the check with which he had paid for it.

In support of this evidence Charles Palm himself was called by the defense and identified the violin as one which he had bought some twelve years before for fifteen or twenty dollars and later sold to Eller. Upon the question of the identity of the instrument then lying before the jury this evidence was conclusive, but, of course, it did not satisfy the jury as to whether Flechter had tried to sell the Palm violin or Bott's violin to Durden. Unfortunately Eller's evidence threw a side light on the defence without which the trial might well have resulted in an acquittal.

Eller had sworn that he was still vigorously endeavoring to get the Palm violin back from Flechter. As contradicting him in this respect, and as tending to show that the suit had not only been compromised but that he and Flechter were engaged in trying to put off the Palm violin as a genuine Stradivarius and share the profit of the fraud, the prosecution introduced the following letter from the witness to his lawyer:

CLIFTON HOUSE, CHICAGO, ILLINOIS.

March 23, 1896.

Dear Counsellor: Received your letter just now. I have been expecting Mr. Flechter's lawyer would settle with you; he got nine hundred dollars for the violin and Mr. Meyer arranged with myself for the half, four hundred and fifty dollars, which he proposed himself and have been expecting a settlement on their part long ago. I have assisted Mr. Palmer, his able lawyer, with the best of my ability, *and have covered Mr. Flechter's shortcomings of faking the violin to a Strad*.

Yours most sincerely,

JOHN ELLER,

Metropolitan Opera Co., Chicago, Ill.

From this letter it was fairly inferable that although the defendant might be innocent of the precise crime with which he was charged, he was, nevertheless, upon his own evidence, guilty of having "faked" a cheap Nicholas violin into a Strad., and of having offered it for sale for the exorbitant price of five thousand dollars. This luckless piece of evidence undoubtedly influenced the jury to convict him.

It will be recalled that ten witnesses for the prosecution had sworn that the violin offered in evidence at the trial was *not* the one produced in the police court, as against the defendant's five who asserted that it *was*.

The testimony was all highly technical and confusing, and the jury probably relied more upon their general impressions of the credibility of the witnesses than upon anything else. It is likely that most of the testimony, on both sides, in regard to the identity of the violin was honestly given, for the question was one upon which a genuine divergence of opinion was easily possible.

Eller's letter from Chicago so affected the jury that they disregarded his testimony and reverted to that of August Gemunder, to whose evidence attention has already been called, and who swore that it was "The Duke of Cambridge" which Flechter had tried to sell to Durden. Alas for the fallibility of even the most honest of witnesses!

The case was ably argued by both sides, and every phase of this curious tangle of evidence given its due consideration. The defense very properly laid stress upon the fact that it would have been a ridiculous performance for Flechter to write the "Cave Dweller" letter and state therein that he was "a violin dealer or maker," thus pointing, unmistakably, to himself, and to further state that for one in his position to dispose of it would be difficult and dangerous. The only explanation for the "Cave Dweller" letter which they could offer, however, was that some one interested in procuring Flechter's downfall had caused it to be sent for that purpose. This might either be a business rival or some one connected with the prosecution.

While Palmer was summing up for the defense he noticed Assistant District Attorney Allen smiling and dramatically turning upon him, he shouted: "This is no laughing matter, Colonel Allen. It is a very serious matter whether this man is to be allowed to-night to go home and kiss his little ones, or whether he is to be cast into jail because you used your brains to concoct a theory against him."

Another consideration, which seemed deserving of weight, was that if Flechter did steal "The Duke of Cambridge" it would have been a piece of incredible folly and carelessness upon his part to leave it in such an exposed place as the safe of his store, where it could be found by the police or shown by the office-boy to any one who called.

Yet the positive identification of August Gemunder and the fatal disclosures of Eller, coupled with the vehement insistence of the prosecution, led the jury to resolve what doubt they had in the case against the prisoner, and, after deliberating eight or ten hours and being out all night, they returned a verdict of guilty. Flechter broke down and declared bitterly that he was the victim of a conspiracy upon the part of his enemies, assisted by a too credulous prosecuting attorney. Everybody admitted that it was an extraordinary case, but the press was consistent in its clamor against Flechter, and opinion generally was that he had been rightly convicted. On May 22nd he was sentenced to the penitentiary for twelve months, but, after being incarcerated in the Tombs for three weeks, he secured a certificate of reasonable doubt and a stay until his conviction could be reviewed on appeal. Then he gave bail and was released. But he had been in jail! Flechter will never forget that! And, for the time being at least, his reputation was gone, his family disgraced, and his business ruined.

A calm reading of the record of the trial suggests that the case abounded in doubts more or less reasonable, and that the Court might well have taken it from the jury on that account. But a printed page of questions and answers carries with it no more than a suggestion of the value of testimony the real significance of which lies in the manner in which it is given, the tone of the voice and the flash of the eye.

Once again Flechter sat at his desk in the window behind the great gilded fiddle. To him, as to its owner, the great Stradivarius had brought only sorrow. But for him the world had no pity. Surely the strains of this wonderful instrument must have had a "dying fall" even when played by the loving hand of old Jean Bott.

At last, after several years, in 1899, the case came up in the Appellate Division of the Supreme Court. Flechter had been led to believe that his conviction would undoubtedly be reversed and a new trial ordered, which would be tantamount to an acquittal, for it was hardly likely in such an event that a second trial would be considered advisable upon the same evidence. But to his great disappointment his conviction was sustained by a divided court, in which only two of the five justices voted for a new trial. Again Fortune had averted her face. If only one more judge had thought the evidence insufficient! The great gilded fiddle seemed to Flechter an omen of misfortune. Once more he gave bail, this time in five thousand dollars, and was set at liberty pending his appeal to the highest court in the State. Once more he took his seat in his office and tried to carry on his business.

But time had dragged on. People had forgotten all about Flechter and the lost Stradivarius, and when his conviction was affirmed little notice was taken of the fact. It was generally assumed that having been sentenced he was in jail.

Then something happened which once more dragged Flechter into the limelight. Editors rushed to their files and dusted the cobwebs off the issues containing the accounts of the trial. The sign of the gilded fiddle became the daily centre of a throng of excited musicians, lawyers and reporters. The lost Stradivarius—the great "Duke of Cambridge"—the nemesis of Bott and of Flechter—was found—by Flechter himself, as he claimed, on August 17, 1900. According to the dealer and his witnesses the amazing discovery occurred in this wise. A violin maker named Joseph Farr, who at one time had worked for Flechter and had testified in his behalf at the trial (to the effect that the instrument produced in the police court was *not* Bott's Stradivarius) saw by chance a very fine violin in the possession of a family named Springer in Brooklyn, and notified Flechter of the fact. The latter, who was always ready to purchase choice violins, after vainly trying for a long time to induce the Springers to bring it to New York, called with Farr upon Mrs. Springer and asked to examine it. To his utter astonishment she produced for his inspection Bott's long-lost Stradivarius. Hardly able to control his excitement Flechter immediately returned to New York and reported the discovery to the police, who instantly began a thorough examination of the circumstances surrounding its discovery.

The District Attorney's office and the Detective Bureau were at first highly suspicious of this opportune discovery on the part of a convicted felon of the precise evidence necessary to clear him, but it was soon demonstrated to their pretty general satisfaction that the famous Stradivarius had in fact been pawned in the shop of one Benjamin Fox on the very day and within an hour of the theft, together with its case and two bows, for the insignificant sum of four dollars. After the legal period of redemption had expired it had been put up at auction and bid in by the pawnbroker for a small advance over the sum for which it had been pawned. It lay exposed for purchase on Fox's shelf for some months, until, in December, 1895, a tailor named James Dooly visited the shop to redeem a silver watch. Being, at the same time, in funds, and able to satisfy his taste as a virtuoso, he felt the need of and bought a violin for ten dollars, but, Fox urging upon him the desirability of getting a good one while he was about it, was finally persuaded to purchase the Bott violin for twenty dollars in its stead. Dooly took it home, played upon it as the spirit moved, and whenever in need of ready money brought it back to Fox as security, always redeeming it in time to prevent its sale. One day, being at Mrs. Springer's, where he was accustomed to purchase tailor trimmings, he offered it to her for sale, and, as her son was taking violin lessons, induced her to buy it for thirty dollars. And in the house of the Springers it had quietly remained ever since, while lawyers and prosecutors wrangled and thundered and witnesses swore positively to the truth, the whole truth and nothing but the truth, to prove that Flechter stole the violin and tried to sell it to Durden.

On these facts, which did not seem to admit of contradiction, Recorder Goff ordered an oral examination of all the witnesses, the hearing of which, sandwiched in between the current trials in his court, dragged along for months, but which finally resulted in establishing to the Court's satisfaction that the violin discovered in the possession of the Springers was the genuine "Duke of Cambridge," and that it could not have been in Flechter's possession at the time he was arrested.

On July 7, 1902, eight years after Bott's death and the arrest and indictment of Flechter for the theft of the violin, a picturesque group assembled in the General Sessions. There was Flechter and his lawyer, Mrs. Springer and her son, the attorneys for the prosecution, and lastly old Mrs. Bott. The seals of the case were broken and the violin identified by the widow as that of her husband. The Springers waived all claim to the violin, and the Court dismissed the indictment against the defendant and ordered the Stradivarius to be delivered to Mrs. Bott, with these words:

"Mrs. Bott, it affords very great pleasure to the Court to give the violin to you. You have suffered many years of sorrow and trouble in regard to it."

"Eight years," sighed the old lady, clasping the violin in her arms.

"I wish you a great deal of pleasure in its possession," continued the Recorder.

Thus ended, as a matter of record, the case of The People against Flechter. For eight years the violin dealer and his family had endured the agony of disgrace, he had spent a fortune in his defense, and had nevertheless been convicted of a crime of which he was at last proved innocent.

Yet, there are those who, when the case is mentioned, shake their heads wisely, as if to say that the whole story of the lost Stradivarius has never been told.

IV
The Last of the Wire-Tappers

"Sir," replied the knave unabashed, "I am one of those who do make a living by their wits."

John Felix, a dealer in automatic musical instruments in New York City, was swindled out of $50,000 on February 2d, 1905, by what is commonly known as the "wire-tapping" game. During the previous August a man calling himself by the name of Nelson had hired Room 46, in a building at 27 East Twenty-second Street, as a school for "wireless telegraphy." Later on he had installed over a dozen deal tables, each fitted with a complete set of ordinary telegraph instruments and connected with wires which, while apparently passing out of the windows, in reality plunged behind a desk into a small "dry" battery. Each table was fitted with a shaded electric drop-light, and the room was furnished with the ordinary paraphernalia of a telegraph office. The janitor never observed any activity in the "school." There seemed to be no pupils, and no one haunted the place except a short, ill-favored person who appeared monthly and paid the rent.

On the afternoon of February 1st, 1905, Mr. Felix was called to the telephone of his store and asked to make an appointment later in the afternoon, with a gentleman named Nelson who desired to submit to him a business proposition. Fifteen minutes afterward Mr. Nelson arrived in person and introduced himself as having met Felix at "Lou" Ludlam's gambling house. He then produced a copy of the *Evening Telegram* which contained an article to the effect that the Western Union Telegraph Company was about to resume its "pool-room service,"—that is to say, to supply the pool rooms with the telegraphic returns of the various horse-races being run in different parts of the United States. The paper also contained, in connection with this item of news, a photograph which might, by a stretch of the imagination, have been taken to resemble Nelson himself.

Mr. Felix, who was a German gentleman of French sympathies, married to an American lady, had recently returned to America after a ten years' sojourn in Europe. He had had an extensive commercial career, was possessed of a considerable fortune, and had at length determined to settle in New York, where he could invest his money to advantage and at the same time conduct a conservative and harmonious business in musical instruments. Like the Teutons of old, dwelling among the forests of the Elbe, Mr. Felix knew the fascination of games of chance and he had heard the merry song of the wheel at both Hambourg and Monte Carlo. In Europe the pleasures of the gaming table had been comparatively inexpensive, but in New York for some unknown reason the fickle goddess had not favored him and he had lost upward of $51,000. "Zu viel!" as he himself expressed it. Being of a philosophic disposition, however, he had pocketed his losses and contented himself with the consoling thought that, whereas he might have lost all, he had in fact lost only a part. It might well have been that had not The Tempter appeared in the person of his afternoon visitor, he would have remained *in status quo* for the rest of his natural life. In the sunny window of his musical store, surrounded by zitherns, auto-harps, dulcimers, psalteries, sackbuts, and other instrument's of melody, the advent of Nelson produced the effect of a sudden and unexpected discord. Felix distrusted him from the very first.

The "proposition" was simplicity itself. It appeared that Mr. Nelson was in the employ of the Western Union Telegraph Company, which had just opened a branch office for racing news at 27 East Twenty-second Street. This branch was under the superintendence of an old associate and intimate friend of Nelson's by the name of McPherson. Assuming that they could find some one with the requisite amount of cash, they could all make their everlasting fortunes by simply having McPherson withhold the news of some race from the pool rooms long enough to allow one of the others to place a large bet upon some horse which had in fact already won and was resting comfortably in the stable. Felix grasped the idea instantly. At the same time he had his suspicions of his visitor. It seemed peculiar that he, an inconspicuous citizen who had already lost $50,000 in gambling houses, should be selected as the recipient of such a momentous opportunity. Moreover, he knew very well that gentlemen in gambling houses were never introduced at all. He thought he detected the odor of a rodent. He naïvely inquired why, if all these things were so, Nelson and his friend were not already yet millionaires two or three times? The answer was at once forthcoming that they *had* been, but also had been robbed—unmercifully robbed, by one in whom they had had confidence and to whom they had entrusted their money.

"And now we are poor, penniless clerks!" sighed Nelson, "and if we should offer to make a big bet ourselves, the gamblers would be suspicious and probably refuse to place it."

"I think this looks like a schvindling game," said Felix shrewdly. So it did; so it was.

By and by Felix put on his hat and, escorted by Nelson, paid a visit to the "branch office" at 27 East Twenty-second Street. Where once solitude had reigned supreme and the spider had spun his web amid the fast-gathering dust, all was now tumultuous activity. Fifteen busy operators in eye shades and shirt sleeves took the news hot from the humming wires and clicked it off to the waiting pool rooms.

"Scarecrow wins by a neck!" cried one, "Blackbird second!"

"Make the odds 5 to 3," shouted a short, ill-favored man, who sat at a desk puffing a large black cigar. The place buzzed like a beehive and ticked like a clockmaker's. It had an atmosphere of breathless excitement all its own. Felix watched and marvelled, wondering if dreams came true.

The short, ill-favored man strolled over and condescended to make Mr. Felix's acquaintance. An hour later the three of them were closeted among the zitherns. At the same moment the fifteen operators were ranged in a line in front, of a neighboring bar, their elbows simultaneously elevated at an angle of forty-five degrees.

Felix still had lingering doubts. Hadn't Mr. McPherson some little paper—a letter, a bill, a receipt or a check, to show that he was really in the employ of the Western Union? No, said "Mac," but he had something better—the badge which he had received as the fastest operator among the company's employees. Felix wanted to see it, but "Mac" explained that it was locked up in the vault at the Farmers' Loan and Trust Co. To Felix this had a safe sound—"Farmers' Trust Co." Then matters began to move rapidly. It was arranged that Felix should go down in the morning and get $50,000 from his bankers, Seligman and Meyer. After that he was to meet Nelson at the store and go with him to the pool room where the big financiers played their money. McPherson was to remain at the "office" and telephone them the results of the races in advance. By nightfall they would be worth half a million.

"I hope you have a good large safe," remarked Nelson, tentatively. The three conspirators parted with mutual expressions of confidence and esteem.

Next morning Mr. Felix went to his bankers and procured $50,000 in five ten-thousand-dollar bills. The day passed very slowly. There was not even a flurry in zitherns. He waited impatiently for Nelson who was to come at five o'clock. At last Nelson arrived and they hurried to the Fifth Avenue Hotel where the *coup* was to take place.

And now another marvel. Wassermann Brothers' stock-brokering office, which closes at three hummed just as the "office" had done the evening before—and with the very same bees, although Felix did not recognize them. It was crowded with men who struggled violently with one another in their eagerness to force their bets into the hands of a benevolent-looking person, who, Felix was informed, was the "trusted cashier" of the establishment. And the sums were so large that even Felix gasped.

"Make that $40,000 on Coco!" cried a bald-headed "capper."

"Mr. Gates wants to double his bet on Jackstone,—make it $80,000!" shrieked another.

"Gentlemen! Gentlemen!" begged the "trusted cashier," "not quite so fast, if you please. One at a time."

"Sixty thousand on Hesper—for a place!" bawled one addressed as "Mr. Keene," while Messrs. "Ryan," "Whitney," "Belmont," "Sullivan," "McCarren," and "Murphy" all made handsome wagers.

From time to time a sporty-looking man standing beside a ticker, shouted the odds and read off the returns. Felix heard with straining ears:

"They're off!"

"Baby leads at the quarter."

"Susan is gaining!"

"They're on the stretch!"

"Satan wins by a nose—Peter second."

There was a deafening uproar, hats were tossed ceilingward, and great wads of money were passed out by the "trusted cashier" to indifferent millionaires. Felix wanted to rush in and bet at once on something—if he waited it might be too late. Was it necessary to be introduced to the cashier? No? Would he take the bet? All right, but—

At that moment a page elbowed his way among the money calling plaintively for "Felix! Mr. Felix." Shrinking at the thought of such publicity in such distinguished company, Felix caught the boy's arm and learned that he was wanted at the telephone booth in the hotel.

"It must be 'Mac,'" said Nelson. "Now don't make any mistake!" Felix promised to use the utmost care.

It was "Mac."

"Is this Mr. Felix?—Yes? Well, be very careful now. I am going to give you the result of the third race which has already been run. I will hold back the news three minutes. This is merely to see if everything is working right. Don't make any bet. If I give you the winners correctly, you can put your money on the fourth race. The horse that won the last is Col. Starbottle—Don Juan is second. Now just step back and see if I am right."

Felix rushed back to the pool room. As he entered the man at the tape was calling out that "they" were off. In due course "they" reached the quarter and then the half. A terrific struggle was in progress between Col. Starbottle and Don Juan. First one was ahead and then the other. Finally they came thundering down to the stretch, Col. Starbottle winning by a neck. "Gates" won $90,000, and several others pocketed wads running anywhere from $20,000 to $60,000.

Felix hurried back to the telephone. "Mac" was at the other end.

"Now write this down," admonished McPherson; "we can't afford to have any mistake. Old Stone has just won the fourth race, with Calvert second. Play Old Stone to win at 5 to 1. We shall make $250,000—and Old Stone is safe in the stable all the time and his jockey is smoking a cigarette on the club house veranda. Good luck, old man."

Felix had some difficulty in getting near the "trusted cashier" so many financiers were betting on Calvert. Felix smiled to himself. He'd show them a thing or two.

Finally he managed to push his envelope containing the five ten-thousand-dollar bills into the "trusted cashier's" hand. The latter marked it "Old Stone, 5 to 1 to win!" and thrust it into his pocket. Then "Whitney" or somebody bet $70,000 on Calvert.

"They're off!" shouted the man at the tape.

How he lived while they tore around the course Felix never knew. Neck and neck Old Stone and Calvert passed the quarter, the half, and the three-quarter post, and with the crowd yelling like demons came hurtling down the stretch.

"Old Stone wins!" cried the "booster" at the tape in a voice husky with excitement. "Calvert a close second!" Felix nearly fainted. His head swam. He had won a quarter of a million. Then the voice of the "booster" made itself audible above the confusion.

"What! A mistake? Not possible!—Yes. Owing to some confusion at the finish, both jockies wearing the same colors, the official returns now read Calvert first; Old Stone second."

Among the zitherns Felix sat and wondered if he had been schvindled. He had not returned to Wassermann Brothers. Had he done so he would have found it empty five minutes after he had lost his money. The millionaires were already streaming hilariously into Sharkey's. "Gates" pledged "Belmont" and "Keene" pledged "Whitney." Each had earned five dollars by the sweat of his brow. The glorious army of wire-tappers had won another victory and their generals had consummated a campaign of months. Expenses (roughly), $600. Receipts, $50,000. Net profits, $48,400. Share of each, $16,133.

A day or two later Felix wandered down to Police Headquarters, and in the Rogue's Gallery identified the photograph of Nelson, whom he then discovered to be none other than William Crane, alias John Lawson, alias John Larsen, a well-known "wire-tapper," arrested some dozen times within a year or two for similar offences. McPherson turned out to be Christopher Tracy, alias Charles J. Tracy, alias Charles Tompkins, alias Topping, alias Toppin, etc., etc., arrested some eight or ten times for "wire-tapping." The "trusted cashier" materialized in the form of one Wyatt, alias, Fred Williams, etc., a "wire-tapper" and pal of "Chappie" Moran and "Larry" Summerfield. Detective Sergeants Fogarty and Mundy were at once detailed upon the case and arrested within a short time both Nelson and McPherson. The "trusted cashier" who had pocketed Felix's $50,000 has never been caught. It is said that he is running a first-class hostelry in a Western city. But that is another story.

When acting Inspector O'Brien ordered McPherson brought into his private room, the latter unhesitatingly admitted that the three of them had "trimmed" Felix of his $50,000, exactly as the latter had alleged. He stated that Wyatt (alias Williams) was the one who had taken in the money, that it was still in his possession, and still intact in its original form. He denied, however, any knowledge of Wyatt's whereabouts.

The reason for this indifference became apparent when the two prisoners were arraigned in the magistrate's court, and their counsel demanded their instant discharge on the ground that they had committed no crime for which they could be prosecuted. He cited an old New York case, McCord vs. The People,[2] which seemed in a general way to sustain his contention, and which had been followed by another and much more recent decision. The People vs. Livingston.[3] The first of these cases had gone to the Court of Appeals, and the general doctrine had been annunciated that where a person parts with his money for an unlawful or dishonest purpose, even though he is tricked into so doing by false pretenses, a prosecution for the crime of larceny cannot be maintained.

[2] 46 New York 470.

[3] 47 App. Div. 283.

In the McCord case, the defendant had falsely pretended to the complainant, a man named Miller, that he was a police officer and held a warrant for his arrest. By these means he had induced Miller to give him a gold watch and a diamond ring as the price of his liberty. The conviction in this case was reversed on the ground that Miller parted with his property for an unlawful purpose; but there was a very strong dissenting opinion from Mr. Justice Peckham, now a member of the bench of the Supreme Court of the United States.

In the second case, that of Livingston, the complainant had been defrauded out of $500 by means of the "green goods" game; but this conviction was reversed by the Appellate Division of the Second Department on the authority of the McCord case. The opinion in this case was written by Mr. justice Cullen, now Chief Judge of the New York Court of Appeals, who says in conclusion:

"We very much regret being compelled to reverse this conviction. Even if the prosecutor intended to deal in counterfeit money, that is no reason why the appellant should go unwhipped of justice. We venture to suggest that it might be Well for the Legislature to alter the rule laid down in McCord vs. People."

Well might the judges regret being compelled to set a rogue at liberty simply because he had been ingenious enough to invent a fraud (very likely with the assistance of a shyster lawyer) which involved the additional turpitude of seducing another into a criminal conspiracy. Livingston was turned loose upon the community in spite of the fact that he had swindled a man out of $500 because he had incidentally led the latter to believe that in return he was to receive counterfeit money or "green goods," which might be put into circulation. Yet, because some years before, the Judges of the Court of Appeals had, in the McCord matter, adopted the rule followed in civil cases, to wit that as the complaining witness was himself in fault and did not come into court with clean hands he could have no standing before them, the Appellate Division in the next case felt obliged to follow them and to rule tantamount to saying that two wrongs could make a right and two knaves one honest man. It may seem a trifle unfair to put it in just this way, but when one realizes the iniquity of such a doctrine as applied to criminal cases, it is hard to speak softly. Thus the broad and general doctrine seemed to be established that so long as a thief could induce his victim to believe that it was to his advantage to enter into a dishonest transaction, he might defraud him to any extent in his power. Immediately there sprang into being hordes of swindlers, who, aided by adroit shyster lawyers, invented all sorts of schemes which involved some sort of dishonesty upon the part of the person to be defrauded. The "wire-tappers," of whom "Larry" Summerfield was the Napoleon, the "gold-brick" and "green-goods" men, and the "sick engineers" flocked to New York, which, under the unwitting protection of the Court of Appeals, became a veritable Mecca for persons of their ilk.

To readers unfamiliar with the cast of mind of professional criminals it will be almost impossible to appreciate with what bold insouciance these vultures now hovered over the metropolitan barnyard. Had not the Court of Appeals itself recognized their profession? They had nothing to fear. The law was on their side. They walked the streets flaunting their immunity in the very face of the police. "Wire-tapping" became an industry, a legalized industry with which the authorities might interfere at their peril. Indeed, there is one instance in which a "wire-tapper" successfully prosecuted his victim (after he had trimmed him) upon a charge of grand larceny arising out of the same transaction. One crook bred another every time he made a victim, and the disease of crime, the most infectious of all distempers, ate its way unchecked into the body politic. Broadway was thronged by a prosperous gentry, the aristocracy and elite of knavery, who dressed resplendently, flourished like the green bay-tree, and spent their (or rather their victims') money with the lavish hand of one of Dumas's gentlemen.

But the evil did not stop there. Seeing that their brothers prospered in New York, and neither being learned in the law nor gifted with the power of nice discrimination between rogueries, all the other knaves in the country took it for granted that they had at last found the Elysian fields and came trooping here by hundreds to ply their various trades. The McCord case stood out like a cabalistic sign upon a gate-post telling all the rascals who passed that way that the city was full of honest folk waiting to be turned into rogues and "trimmed."

"And presently we did pass a narrow lane, and at the mouth espied a written stone, telling beggars by a word like a wee pitchfork to go that way."

The tip went abroad that the city was "good graft" for everybody, and in the train of the "wire-tappers" thronged the "flimflammer," "confidence man," "booster," "capper" and every sort of affiliated crook, recalling Charles Reade's account in "The Cloister and the Hearth" of Gerard in Lorraine among their kin of another period:

With them and all they had, 'twas lightly come and lightly go; and when we left them my master said to me, "This is thy first lesson, but to-night we shall be at Hansburgh. Come with me to the 'rotboss' there, and I'll show thee all our folk and their lays, and especially 'the lossners,' 'the dutzers,' 'the schleppers,' 'the gickisses,' 'the schwanfelders,' whom in England we call 'shivering Jemmies,' 'the süntregers,' 'the schwiegers,' 'the joners,' 'the sessel-degers,' 'the gennscherers,' in France 'marcandiers a rifodés,' 'the veranerins,' 'the stabulers,' with a few foreigners like ourselves, such as 'pietres,' 'francmitoux,' 'polissons,' 'malingreux,' 'traters,' 'rufflers,' 'whipjacks,' 'dommerars,' 'glymmerars,' 'jarkmen,' 'patricos,' 'swadders,' 'autem morts,' 'walking morts,'—" "Enow!" cried I, stopping him, "art as gleesome as the evil one a counting of his imps. I'll jot down in my tablet all these caitiffs and their accursed names: for knowledge is knowledge. But go among them alive or dead, that will I not with my good will."

And a large part of it was due simply to the fact that seven learned men upon seven comfortable chairs in the city of Albany had said, many years ago, that "neither the law or public policy designs the protection of rogues in their dealings with each other, or to insure fair dealing and truthfulness as between each other, in their dishonest practices."

The reason that the "wire-tapping" game was supposed to come within the scope of the McCord case was this: it deluded the victim into the belief that he was going to cheat the pool room by placing a bet upon a "sure thing." Secondarily it involved, as the dupe supposed, the theft or disclosure of messages which were being transmitted over the lines of a telegraph company—a misdemeanor. Hence, it was argued, the victim was as much a thief as the proposer of the scheme, had parted with his money for a dishonest purpose, did not come into court with "clean hands," and no prosecution could be sustained, no matter whether he had been led to give up his money by means of false pretenses or not.

While "wire-tapping" differed technically from the precise frauds committed by McCord and Livingston, it nevertheless closely resembled those swindlers in general character and came clearly within the doctrine that the law was not designed to protect "rogues in their dealings with each other."

No genuine attempt had ever been made to prosecute one of these gentry until the catastrophe which deprived Felix of his $50,000. The "wire-tappers" rolled in money. Indeed, the fraternity were so liberal with their "rolls" that they became friendly with certain police officials and intimately affiliated with various politicians of influence, a friend of one of whom went on Summerfield's bond, when the latter was being prosecuted for the "sick-engineer" frauds to the extent of $30,000. They regularly went to Europe in the summer season and could be seen at all the race-courses and gambling resorts of the Continent. It is amusing to chronicle in this connection that just prior to McPherson's arrest—that is to say during the summer vacation of 1904—he crossed the Atlantic on the same steamer with an assistant district attorney of New York county, who failed to recognize his ship companion and found him an entertaining and agreeable comrade.

The trial came on before Judge Warren W. Foster in Part 3 of the General Sessions on February 27th, 1906. A special panel quickly supplied a jury, which, after hearing the evidence, returned in short order a verdict of guilty. As Judge Foster believed the McCord case to be still the law of the State, he, of his own motion, and with commendable independence, immediately arrested judgment. The People thereupon appealed, the Court of Appeals sustained Judge Foster, and the defendant was discharged. It is, however, satisfactory to record that the Legislature at its next session amended the penal code in such a way as to entirely deprive the wire-tappers and their kind of the erstwhile protection which they had enjoyed under the law.

V
The Franklin Syndicate

When Robert A. Ammon, a member of the New York bar, was convicted, after a long trial, on the 17th of June, 1903, of receiving stolen goods, he had, in the parlance of his class, been "due" for a long time. The stolen property in question was the sum of thirty thousand five hundred dollars in greenbacks, part of the loot of the notorious "Franklin Syndicate," devised and engineered by William F. Miller, who later became the catspaw of his legal adviser, the subject of this history.

Ammon stood at the bar and listened complacently to his sentence of not less than four years at hard labor in Sing Sing. A sneer curved his lips as, after nodding curtly to his lawyer, he turned to be led away by the court attendant. The fortune snatched from his client had procured for him the most adroit of counsel, the most exhaustive of trials. He knew that nothing had been left undone to enable him to evade the consequences of his crime, and he was cynically content.

For years "Bob" Ammon had been a familiar figure in the Wall Street district of New York. Although the legal adviser of swindlers and confidence men, he was a type of American whose energies, if turned in a less dubious direction, might well have brought him honorable distinction. Tall, strong as a bull, bluff, good-natured, reckless and of iron nerve, he would have given good account of himself as an Indian fighter or frontiersman. His fine presence, his great vitality, his coarse humor, his confidence and bravado, had won for him many friends of a certain kind and engendered a feeling among the public that somehow, although the associate and adviser of criminals, he was outside the law, to the circumventing of which his energies were directed. Unfortunately his experiences with the law had bred in him a contempt for it which ultimately caused his downfall.

"The reporters arc bothering you, are they?" he had said to Miller in his office. "Hang them! Send them to me. I'll talk to them!"

And talk to them he did. He could talk a police inspector or a city magistrate into a state of vacuous credulity, and needless to say he was to his clients as a god knowing both good and evil, as well as how to eschew the one and avoid the other. Miller hated, loathed and feared him, yet freely entrusted his liberty, and all he had risked his liberty to gain, to this strange and powerful personality which held him enthralled by the mere exercise of a physical superiority.

The "Franklin Syndicate" had collapsed amid the astonished outcries of its thousands of victims, on November 24th, 1899, when, under the advice and with the assistance of Ammon, its organizer, "520 per cent. Miller," had fled to Canada. It was nearly four years later, in June, 1903, that Ammon, arraigned at the bar of justice as a criminal, heard Assistant District Attorney Nott call William F. Miller, convict, to the stand to testify against him. A curious contrast they presented as they faced one another; the emaciated youth of twenty-five, the hand of Death already tightly fastened upon his meagre frame, coughing, hollow-cheeked, insignificant, flat-nosed, almost repulsive, who dragged himself to the witness chair, and the swaggering athlete who glared at him from the bar surrounded by his cordon of able counsel. As Ammon fixed his penetrating gaze upon his former client, Miller turned pale and dropped his eyes. Then the prosecutor, realizing the danger of letting the old hypnotic power return, even for an instant, quickly stepped between them. Miller raised his eyes and smiled, and those who heard knew that this miserable creature had been through the fire and come forth to speak true things.

The trial of Ammon involved practically the reproving of the case against Miller, for which the latter had been convicted and sentenced to ten years in State's prison, whence he now issued like one from the tomb to point the skeleton, incriminating finger at his betrayer. But the case began by the convict-witness testifying that the whole business was a miserable fraud from start to finish, carried on and guided by the advice of the defendant. He told how he, a mere boy of twenty-one, burdened with a sick wife and baby, unfitted by training or ability for any sort of lucrative employment, a hanger-on of bucket shops and, in his palmiest days, a speculator in tiny lots of feebly margined stocks, finding himself without means of support, conceived the alluring idea of soliciting funds for investment, promising enormous interest, and paying this interest out of the principal intrusted to him. For a time he preyed only upon his friends, claiming "inside information" of large "deals" and paying ten per cent. per week on the money received out of his latest deposits.

Surely the history of civilization is a history of credulity. Miller prospered. His earlier friend-customers who had hesitatingly taken his receipt for ten dollars, and thereafter had received one dollar every Monday morning, repeated the operation and returned in ever-increasing numbers. From having his office "in his hat," he took an upper room in a small two-story house at 144 Floyd Street, Brooklyn—an humble tenement, destined to be the scene of one of the most extraordinary exhibitions of man's cupidity and foolishness in modern times. At first he had tramped round, like a pedler, delivering the dividends himself and soliciting more, but soon he hired a boy. This was in February, 1899. Business increased. The golden flood began to appear in an attenuated but constant rivulet. He hired four more employees and the whole top floor of the house. The golden rivulet became a steady stream. From a "panhandler" he rolled in ready thousands. The future opened into magnificent auriferous distances. He began to call himself "The Franklin Syndicate," and to advertise that "the way to wealth is as plain as the road to the market." He copied the real brokers and scattered circulars and "weekly letters" over the country, exciting the rural mind in distant Manitoba and Louisiana.

There was an instantaneous response. His mail required the exclusive attention of several clerks. The stream of gold became a rushing torrent. Every Monday morning the Floyd Street house was crowded with depositors who drew their interest, added to it, deposited it again, and went upon their way rejoicing. Nobody was going to have to work any more. The out-of-town customers received checks for their interest drawn upon "The Franklin Syndicate," together with printed receipts for their deposits, all signed "William F. Miller," by means of a rubber stamp. No human hand could have signed them all without writer's cramp. The rubber stamp was Miller's official signature. Then with a mighty roar the torrent burst into a deluge. The Floyd Street quarters were besieged by a clamoring multitude fighting to see which of them could give up his money first, and there had to be a special delivery for Miller's mail. He rented the whole house and hired fifty clerks. You could deposit your money almost anywhere, from the parlor to the pantry, the clothes closet or the bath-room. Fridays the public stormed the house *en masse*, since the money must be deposited *on that day* to draw interest for the following week. The crush was so enormous that the stoop broke down. Imagine it! In quiet Brooklyn! People struggling to get up the steps to cram their money into Miller's pockets! There he sat, behind a desk, at the top of the stoop, solemnly taking the money thrown down before him and handing out little pink and green stamped receipts in exchange. There was no place to put the money, so it was shoved on to the floor behind him. Friday afternoons Miller and his clerks waded through it, knee high. There was no pretense of bookkeeping. Simply in self-defense Miller issued in October a pronunciamento that he could not in justice to his business, consent to receive less than fifty dollars at one time. Theoretically, there was no reason why the thing should not have gone on practically forever, Miller and everybody else becoming richer and richer. So long as the golden stream swelled five times each year everybody would be happy. How could anybody fail to be happy who saw so much money lying around loose everywhere?

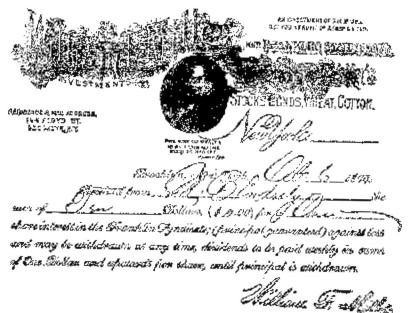

One of Miller's Franklin Syndicate Receipts.

But the business had increased to such an extent that Miller began to distrust his own capacity to handle it. He therefore secured a partner in the person of one Edward Schlessinger, and with him went to Charlestown, Mass., for the purpose of opening another office, in charge of which they placed a man named Louis Powers. History repeated itself. Powers shipped the deposits to Miller every day or two by express. Was there ever such a plethora of easy money?

But Schlessinger was no Miller. He decided that he must have a third of the profits (Heaven knows how they computed them!) and have them, moreover, each day *in cash*. Hence there was a daily accounting, part of the receipts being laid aside to pay off interest checks and interest, and the balance divided. Schlessinger carried his off in a bag; Miller took the rest, cash, money orders and checks, and deposited it in a real bank. How the money poured in may be realized from the fact that the excess of receipts over disbursements for the month ending November 16th was four hundred and thirty thousand dollars.

Hitherto Miller had been the central figure. Col. Robert A. Ammon now became the *deus ex machina*. Miller's advertising had become so extensive that he had been forced to retain a professional agent, one Rudolph Guenther, to supervise it, and when the newspapers began to make unpleasant comments, Guenther took Miller to Ammon's office in the Bennett Building in Nassau Street. Ammon accepted a hundred dollars from Miller, listened to his account of the business and examined copies of the circulars. When he was handed one of the printed receipts he said they were "incriminating." Miller must try to get them back. He advised (as many another learned counsellor has done) incorporating the business, since by this means stock could be sold and exchanged for the incriminating receipts. He explained the mistakes of the "*Dean* crowd," but showed how he had been able to safeguard them in spite of the fact that they had foolishly insisted on holding the stock in their company themselves instead of making their customers the stockholders. Nevertheless "you do not see any of the Dean people in jail," boasted Ammon. From now on Miller and he were in frequent consultation, and Ammon took steps to incorporate, procuring for that purpose from Wells, Fargo & Co. a certificate of deposit for one hundred thousand dollars. Occasionally he would visit Floyd Street to see how things were going. Miller became a mere puppet; Ammon twitched the wire.

It was now well on in November, and the press of both Boston and New York was filled with scathing attacks upon the Syndicate. The reporters became so inquisitive as to be annoying to the peaceful Miller. "Send the reporters over to me!" directed Ammon.

The *Post* (of Boston) said the whole thing was a miserable swindle. Ammon, accompanied by Miller, carrying a satchel which contained fifty thousand dollars in greenbacks, went to Boston, visited the offices of the *Post*, and pitched into the editor.

"The business is all right; you must give us a fair deal!"

The pair also visited Watts, the chief of police.

"You keep your mouth shut," said Ammon to Miller. "I'll do all the talking." He showed Watts the bag of money, and demanded what he had meant by calling the enterprise a "green goods business." If the thing wasn't all right, did Watts suppose that he, Col. Robert A. Ammon, would be connected with it? The chief backed down, and explained that he had jokingly referred to the color of one of the receipts—which happened to be green.

In spite of Ammon's confidence, however, there was an uneasy feeling in the air, and it was decided to put an advertisement in the *Post* offering to allow any customer who so desired to withdraw his deposit, *without notice*, upon the following Saturday. This announcement did not have precisely the anticipated effect, and Saturday saw a large crowd of victims eager to withdraw their money from the Boston office of the Franklin Syndicate. Powers paid the "*Pauls*," of Boston, out of the bag brought on by Miller containing the deposits of the "*Peters*," of Brooklyn. Meantime, Ammon addressed the throng, incidentally blackguarding a *Post* reporter before the crowd, telling them that his paper was a "yellow paper, had never amounted to anything, and never would." Some timid souls took courage and redeposited their money. The run continued one day and cost Ammon and Miller about twenty-eight thousand dollars. Ammon took five thousand dollars cash as a fee out of the bag, and the pair returned to New York. But confidence had been temporarily restored.

The beginning of the end, however, was now in sight—at least for the keen vision of Bob Ammon. He advised stimulating deposits and laying hands on all the money possible before the crash came. Accordingly Miller sent a telegram (collect) to all depositors:

We have inside information of a big transaction, to begin Saturday or Monday morning. Big profits. Remit at once so as to receive the profits.

WILLIAM F. MILLER,

Franklin Syndicate.

A thousand or so were returned, the depositors having refused to pay the charges. The rest of the customers in large measure responded. But the game was nearly up. There were scare-heads in the papers. Miller saw detectives on every corner, and, like a rat leaving a sinking ship, Schlessinger scuttled away for the last time with a bag of money on the evening of Tuesday, November 21st, 1899. The rest of the deposits were crammed into Miller's desk and left there over night.

The next morning Miller returned to Floyd Street and spent that day in the usual routine, and also on Thursday remained until about twelve o'clock noon, when he placed thirty thousand five hundred dollars in bills in a satchel and started for Ammon's office, where he found Schlessinger—likewise with a satchel.

"The jig's up," announced Schlessinger.

"Billy, I think you'll have to make a run for it," said Ammon. "The best thing for you is to go to Canada."

It still remained to secure the money, which Miller had deposited in the banks, in such a way that the customers could not get hold of it. Ammon explained how that could easily be done. The money should be all turned over to him, and none of the creditors would ever see it again. He did not deem it necessary to suggest that neither would Miller. Accordingly the two, the lawyer and the client, went to the office of Wells, Fargo & Co., Ammon obligingly carrying the satchel containing the thirty thousand five hundred dollars. Here Ammon deposited the contents to his own account, as well as the certificate of deposit for one hundred thousand dollars previously mentioned, and a check for ten thousand dollars, representing the balance of Miller's loot. In addition to this he received an order for forty thousand dollars United States Government bonds, which were on deposit with Wells, Fargo & Co., and later, through Miller's father, sixty-five thousand dollars in bonds of the New York Central Railroad and the United States Government. Thus Ammon secured from his dupe the sum of two hundred and forty-five thousand five hundred dollars, the actual market value of the securities bringing the amount up to two hundred and fifty thousand five hundred dollars, besides whatever sums he had been paid by Miller for legal services, which could not have been less than ten or fifteen thousand dollars. The character of the gentleman is well illustrated by the fact that later when paying Mrs. Miller her miserable pittance of five dollars per week, he explained to her that "he was giving her that out of his own money, and that her husband *owed him*."

Ammon's deposit slips and a receipt signed by Mrs. Ammon.

There still remained, however, the chance of getting a few dollars more and Ammon advised Miller "to try to get Friday's receipts, which were the heaviest day's business." Acting on this suggestion, Miller returned to Floyd Street the next morning at about half past nine, finding a great crowd of people waiting outside. About one o'clock he started to go home, but discovering that he was being followed by a man whom he took to be a detective, he boarded a street car, dodged through a drug store and a Chinese laundry, finally made the elevated railroad, with his pursuer at his heels, and eventually reached the lawyer's office about two o'clock in the afternoon. Word was received almost immediately over the telephone that Miller had been indicted in Kings County for conspiracy to defraud, and Ammon stated that the one thing for Miller to do was to go away. Miller replied that he did not want to go unless he could take his wife and baby with him, but Ammon assured him that he would send them to Canada later in charge of his own wife. Under this promise Miller agreed to go, and Ammon procured a man named Enright to take Miller to Canada, saying that "he was an ex-detective and could get him out of the way." Ammon further promised to forward to Miller whatever money he might need to retain lawyers for him in Montreal. Thereupon Miller exchanged hats with some one in Ammon's office and started for Canada in the custody of the lawyer's representative.

How the wily colonel must have chuckled as poor Miller trotted down the stairs like a sheep leaving his fleece behind him. A golden fleece indeed! Did ever a lawyer have such a piece of luck? Here was a little fellow who had invented a brilliant scheme to get away with other people's money and had carried it through successfully—more than successfully, beyond the dreams of even the most avaricious criminal, and then, richer than Midas, had handed over the whole jolly fortune to another for the other's asking, without even taking a scrap of paper to show for it. More than that, he had then voluntarily extinguished himself. Had Ammon not chuckled he would not have been Bob Ammon. The money was stolen, to be sure, but Ammon's skirts were clear. There was nothing to show that the two hundred and forty-five thousand dollars he had received was stolen money. There was only one man—a discredited felon, who could hint that the money was even "tainted," and *he* was safely over the border, in a foreign jurisdiction, not in the custody of the police, but of Ammon himself, to be kept there (as Mr. Robert C. Taylor so aptly phrased it in arguing Ammon's case on appeal) "on waiting orders. Ammon had Miller on a string, and as soon as Ammon (for his own sake) was compelled either to produce Miller or to run the risk of indictment, he pulled the string and brought Miller back into the jurisdiction."

Needless to say great was the ado made over the disappearance of the promoter of the Franklin Syndicate, and the authorities of King's County speedily let it become known that justice required that some one should be punished for the colossal fraud which had been perpetrated. The grand jury of the county started a general investigation. Public indignation was stirred to the point of ebullition. In the midst of the rumpus, there came a knock on the office door of the Hon. John F. Clark, District Attorney of King's County, and Col. Robert A. Ammon announced himself. The two men were entire strangers to each other but this did not prevent Ammon, with his inimitable assurance, from addressing the District Attorney by his first name.

"How are you, John?" he inquired nonchalantly, "what can I do for you?"

Mr. Clark repressed his natural inclination to kick the insolent fellow forcibly out of his office, invited him to be seated and rang for a stenographer. Ammon asserted his anxiety to assist the District Attorney by every means in his power, but denied knowing the whereabouts of Miller, alleging that he was simply acting as his counsel. Mr. Clark replied that in Miller's absence the grand jury might take the view that Ammon himself was the principal. At this Ammon calmly assured his host that as far as he was concerned he was ready to go before the grand jury at any time.

"That is just what I want," returned Mr. Clark, "the grand jury is in session. Come over."

Ammon arose with a smile and accompanied the District Attorney towards the door of the grand jury room. Just outside he suddenly placed his hand to his head as if recollecting something.

"One moment," he exclaimed. "I forgot that I have an engagement. I will come over to-morrow."

"Ah!" retorted Mr. Clark, "I do not think you will be here to-morrow."

Two weeks later Miller was safely ensconced without bail in Raymond Street jail.

Schlessinger, who got away with one hundred and seventy-five thousand dollars in cash, fled to Europe where he lived high, frequenting the race tracks and gaming tables until he was called to his final account a year or two ago. The money which he took has never been traced. Miller was tried, convicted and sent to Sing Sing. The Appellate Division of the Supreme Court then reversed his conviction, but later, on appeal to the Court of Appeals, it was sustained.

Of the enormous sums turned over to Ammon Miller received nothing save the money necessary for his support in Montreal, for the lawyers who defended him, and five dollars per week for his wife and child up to the time he turned State's evidence. It is interesting to note that among the counsel representing Miller upon his trial was Ammon himself. Miller's wife and child were not sent to Montreal by Ammon, nor did the latter secure bail for his client at any time during his different periods of incarceration. The colonel knew very well that it was a choice between himself and Miller and took no steps which might necessitate the election falling upon himself.

The conviction of Miller, with his sentence to ten years in State's prison did not, however, prevent the indictment of Ammon for receiving stolen money in New York County, although the chance that he would ever have to suffer for his crime seemed small indeed. The reader must bear in mind that up to the time of Ammon's trial Miller had never admitted his guilt; that he was still absolutely, and apparently irrevocably, under Ammon's sinister influence, keeping in constant communication with him and implicitly obeying his instructions while in prison; and that Miller's wife and child were dependent upon Ammon for their daily bread. No wonder Ammon strode the streets confident that his creature would never betray him.

"Now, Billy, you don't want to be shooting off your mouth up here," was his parting injunction to his dupe on his final visit to Sing Sing before he became a guest there himself at the expense of the People.

Miller followed his orders to the letter, and the stipend was increased to the munificent sum of forty dollars per month.

Meantime the case against Ammon languished and the District Attorney of New York County was at his wits' end to devise a means to procure the evidence to convict him. To do this it would be necessary to establish affirmatively that the thirty thousand five hundred dollars received by Ammon from Miller and deposited with Wells, Fargo & Co. was the identical money stolen by Miller from the victims of the Franklin Syndicate. It was easy enough to prove that Miller stole hundreds of thousands of dollars, that Ammon received hundreds of thousands, but you had to prove that the same money stolen by Miller passed to the hands of Ammon. Only one man in the world, as Ammon had foreseen, could supply this last necessary link in the chain of evidence and he was a convict—and mute.

It now became the task of the District Attorney to induce Miller to confess the truth and take the stand against Ammon. He had been in prison a considerable time and his health was such as to necessitate his being transferred to the hospital ward. Several of the District Attorney's assistants visited him at various times at Sing Sing in the hope of being able to persuade him to turn State's evidence, but all their efforts were in vain. Miller refused absolutely to say anything that would tend to implicate Ammon.

At last the District Attorney himself, accompanied by Mr. Nott, who later prosecuted Ammon, made a special trip to Sing Sing to see what could be done. They found Miller lying upon his prison pallet, his harsh cough and blazing eyes speaking only too patently of his condition. At first Mr. Nott tried to engage him in conversation while the District Attorney occupied himself with other business in another part of the ward, but it was easily apparent that Miller would say nothing. The District Attorney then approached the bed where Miller was lying and inquired if it were true that he declined to say anything which might tend to incriminate Ammon. After some hesitation Miller replied that, even if he should testify against his old accomplice, there was nothing to show that he would be pardoned, and that he would not talk unless he had actually in his hands some paper or writing which would guarantee that if he did so he would be set free.

The spectacle of a convicted felon haggling with an officer of the law over the terms upon which he would consent to avail himself of an opportunity to make the only reparation still possible angered the District Attorney, and, turning fiercely upon the prisoner, he arraigned him in scathing terms, stating that he was a miserable swindler and thief, who had robbed thousands of poor people of all the money they had in the world, that he showed himself devoid of every spark of decency or repentance by refusing to assist the law in punishing his confederate and assisting his victims in getting back what was left of the money, and that he, the District Attorney, felt himself humiliated in having consented to come there to visit and talk with such a heartless and depraved specimen of humanity. The District Attorney then turned his back upon Miller, whose eyes filled with tears, but who made no response.

A few moments later the convict asked permission to speak to the District Attorney alone. With some reluctance the latter granted the request and the others drew away.

"Mr. District Attorney," said the wretched man in a trembling voice, with the tears still suffusing his eyes, "I *am* a thief; I did rob all those poor people, and I am heartily sorry for it. I would gladly die, if by doing so I could pay them back. But I haven't a single cent of all the money that I stole and the only thing that stands between my wife and baby and starvation is my keeping silence. If I did what you ask, the only money they have to live on would be stopped. I can't see them starve, glad as I would be to do what I can now to make up for the wrong I have done."

The District Attorney's own eyes were not entirely dry as he held out his hand to Miller.

"Miller," he replied, "I have done you a great injustice. I honor you for the position you have taken. Were I in your place I should probably act exactly as you are doing. I cannot promise you a pardon if you testify against Ammon. I cannot even promise that your wife will receive forty dollars a month, for the money in my charge cannot be used for such a purpose; all I can assure you of is that, should you decide to help me, a full and fair statement of all you may have done will be sent to the Governor with a request that he act favorably upon any application for a pardon which you may make. The choice must be your own. Whatever you decide to do, you have my respect and sympathy. Think well over the matter. Do not decide at once; wait for a day or two, and I will return to New York and you can send me word."

The next day Miller sent word that he had determined to tell the truth and take the stand, whatever the consequences to himself and his family might be. He was immediately transferred to the Tombs Prison in New York City, where he made a complete and full confession, not only assisting in every way in securing evidence for the prosecution of Ammon, but aiding his trustee in bankruptcy to determine the whereabouts of some sixty thousand dollars of the stolen money, which but for him would never have been recovered. At the same time Ammon was re-arrested upon a bench warrant, and his bail sufficiently increased to render his appearance for trial probable. As Miller had foreseen, the monthly payment to his wife instantly stopped.

The usual effect produced upon a jury by the testimony of a convict accomplice is one of distrust or open incredulity. Every word of Miller's story, however, carried with it the impression of absolute truth. As he proceeded, in spite of the sneers of the defence, an extraordinary wave of sympathy for the man swept over the court-room, and the jury listened with close attention to his graphic account of the rise and fall of the outrageous conspiracy which had attempted to shield its alluring offer of instant wealth behind the name of America's most practical philosopher, whose only receipt for the same end had been frugality and industry. Supported as Miller was by the corroborative testimony of other witnesses and by the certificates of deposit which Ammon had, with his customary bravado, made out in his own handwriting, no room was left for even the slightest doubt, not only that the money had been stolen but that Ammon had received it. Indeed so plain was the proposition that the defence never for an instant contemplated the possibility of putting Ammon upon the stand in his own behalf. It was in truth an extraordinary case, for the principal element in the proof was made out by the evidence of the thief himself that he was a thief. Miller had been tried and convicted of the very larceny to which he now testified, and, although in the eyes of the law no principle of res adjudicata could apply in Ammon's case, it was a logical conclusion that if the evidence upon the first trial was repeated, the necessary element of larceny would be effectually established. Hence, in point of fact,

Miller's testimony upon the question of whether the money had been *stolen* was entirely unnecessary, and the efforts of the defence were directed simply to making out Miller such a miscreant upon his own testimony that perforce the jury could not accept his evidence when it reached the point of implicating Ammon. All their attempts in this direction, however, only roused increased sympathy for the witness and hostility toward their own client, and made the jury the more ready to believe that Ammon had been the only one in the end to profit by the transaction.

Briefly, the two points urged by the defence were:

(1) That Ammon was acting only as Miller's counsel, and hence was immune, and,

(2) That there was no adequate legal evidence that the thirty thousand five hundred dollars which Ammon had deposited, as shown by the deposit slip, was the identical money stolen from the victims of the Franklin syndicate. As bearing upon this they urged that the stolen money had in fact been deposited by Miller himself, and so had lost the character of stolen money before it was turned over to the defendant, and that Miller's story being that of an accomplice required absolute corroboration in every detail.

The point that Ammon was acting only as a lawyer was quickly disposed of by Judge Newburger.

"Something has been said by counsel," he remarked in his charge to the jury, "to the effect that the defendant, as a lawyer, had a perfect right to advise Miller, but I know of no rule of law that will permit counsel to advise how a crime can be committed."

As to the identity of the money, the Court charged that it made no difference which person performed the physical act of placing the cash in the hands of the receiving teller of the bank, so long as it was deposited to Ammon's credit.

On the question of what corroboration of Miller's story was necessary, Judge Ingraham, in the Appellate Division, expressed great doubt as to whether in the eyes of the law Miller, the thief, could be regarded as an accomplice of Ammon in receiving the stolen money at all, and stated that even if he could be so regarded, there was more than abundant corroboration of his testimony.

Ammon's conviction was affirmed throughout the courts, including the Court of Appeals, and the defendant himself is now engaged in serving out his necessarily inadequate sentence—necessarily inadequate, since under the laws of the State of New York, the receiver of stolen goods, however great his moral obliquity may be, and however great the amount stolen, can only receive half the punishment which may be meted out to the thief himself, "receiving" being punishable by only five years or less in State's prison, while grand larceny is punishable by ten years.

Yet who was the greater criminal—the weak, ignorant, poverty-stricken clerk, or the shrewd, experienced lawyer who preyed upon his client and through him upon the community at large?

The confession of Miller, in the face of what the consequences of his course might mean to his wife and child, was an act of moral courage. The price he had to pay is known to himself alone. But the horrors of life in prison for the "squealer" were thoroughly familiar to him when he elected to do what he could to atone for his crime. In fact Ammon had not neglected to picture them vividly to him and to stigmatize an erstwhile client of his.

"Everything looks good," he wrote to Miller in Sing Sing, in reporting the affirmance of Goslin's conviction, "especially since the *squealer* is getting his just *deserts*."

With no certain knowledge of a future pardon Miller went back to prison cheerfully to face all the nameless tortures inflicted upon those who help the State—the absolute black silence of convict excommunication, the blows and kicks inflicted without opportunity for retaliation or complaint, the hostility of guards and keepers, the suffering of abject poverty, keener in a prison house than on any other foot of earth.

It is interesting to observe that Miller's original purpose had been to secure money to speculate with—for he had been bitten deep by the tarantula of Wall Street, and his early experiences had led him to believe that he could beat the market if only he had sufficient margin. This margin he set out to secure. Then when he saw how easy it was to get money for the asking, he dropped the idea of speculation and simply became a banker. He did make one bona-fide attempt, but the stock went down, he sold out and netted a small loss. Had Miller actually *continued to speculate* it is doubtful whether he could have been convicted for any crime, since it was for that purpose that the money was entrusted to him. He might have lost it all in the Street and gone scot free. As it was, in failing to gamble with it, he became guilty of embezzlement.

Ammon arrived in Sing Sing with a degree of éclat. He found numerous old friends and clients among the inmates. He brought a social position which had its value. Money, too, is no less desirable there than elsewhere, and Ammon had plenty of it.

In due course, but not until he had served more than half his sentence (less commutation), Miller a broken man, received his pardon, and went back to his wife and child. When Governor Higgins performed this act of executive clemency, many honest folk in Brooklyn and elsewhere loudly expressed their indignation. District Attorney Jerome did not escape their blame. Was this contemptible thief, this meanest of all mean swindlers, who had stolen hundreds of thousands to be turned loose on the community before he had served half his sentence? It was an outrage! A disgrace to civilization! Reader, how say you?

VI
A Study in Finance

"He that maketh haste to be rich shall not be innocent."—PROVERBS 28:20.

The victim of moral overstrain is the central figure in many novels and countless magazine stories. In most of them he finally repents him fully of his sins past and returns to his former or to some equally desirable position, to lead a new and better life. The dangers and temptations of the "Street" are, however, too real and terrible to be studied other than in actuality, and the fall of hundreds of previously honest young men owing to easily remedied conditions should teach its lesson, not only to their comrades, but to their employers as well. The ball and chain, quite as often as repentance and forgiveness, ends their experience.

No young man takes a position in a banking-house with the deliberate intention of becoming an embezzler. He knows precisely, as well as does the reader, that if he listens to the whisper of temptation he is lost—and so does his employer. Yet the employer, who would hold himself remiss if he allowed his little boy to have the run of the jam-closet and then discovered that the latter's lips bore evidence of petty larceny, or would regard himself as almost criminally negligent if he placed a priceless pearl necklace where an ignorant chimney-sweep might fall under the hypnotism of its shimmer, will calmly allow a condition of things in his own brokerage or banking office where a fifteen-dollars-a-week clerk may have free access to a million dollars' worth of negotiable securities, and even encourage the latter by occasional "sure" tips to take a flyer in the market.

It is a deplorable fact that the officers of certain companies occasionally "unload" undesirable securities upon their employees, and, in order to boom or create a "movement" in a certain stock, will induce the persons under their control to purchase it. It would be a rare case in which a clerk who valued his situation would refuse to take a few shares in an enterprise which the head of the firm was fathering. Of course, such occurrences are the exceptions, but there are plenty of houses not far from Wall Street where the partners know that their clerks and messengers are "playing the market," and exert not the slightest influence to stop them. When these men find that they and their customers, and not the clerks and messengers, are paying the loss accounts of the latter, they are very much distressed, and tell the District Attorney, with regret, that only by sending such wicked and treacherous persons to State's prison can similar dishonesty be prevented.

Not long ago the writer became acquainted with a young man who, as loan clerk in a trust company, had misappropriated a large amount of securities and had pleaded guilty to the crime of grand larceny in the first degree. He was awaiting sentence, and in connection therewith it became necessary to examine into the conditions prevailing generally in the financial district. His story is already public property, for the case attracted wide attention in the daily press; but, inasmuch as the writer's object is to point a moral rather than adorn a tale, the culprit's name and the name of the company with which he was connected need not be given.

He is now serving a term in State's prison and is, the writer believes, sincerely repentant and determined to make a man of himself upon his release. For present purposes let him be called John Smith. He was born in New York City, in surroundings rather better than the average. His family were persons of good education and his home was a comfortable and happy one. From childhood he received thorough religious instruction and was always a straightforward, honest and obedient boy. His father, having concluded from observation that the shortest route to success lay in financial enterprise, secured a place in a broker's office for his son after the latter's graduation from the high school. John began at the bottom and gradually worked up to the position of assistant loan clerk in a big trust company. This took fifteen years of hard work.

From the day that he started in filling inkwells and cleaning out ticker baskets, he saw fortunes made and lost in a twinkling. He learned that the chief business of a broker is acting as go-between for persons who are trying to sell what they do not own to others who have not the money to pay for what they buy. And he saw hundreds of such persons grow rich on these fictitious transactions. He also saw others "wiped out," but they cheerfully went through bankruptcy and began again, many of them achieving wealth on their second or third attempt. He was earning five dollars a week and getting his lunch at a "vegetarian health restaurant" for fifteen cents. The broker, for whom he ran errands, gave away thirty-five-cent cigars to his customers and had an elaborate luncheon served in the office daily to a dozen or more of the elect. John knew one boy of about his own age, who, having made a successful turn, began as a trader and cleaned up a hundred thousand dollars in a rising market the first year. That was better than the cleaning up John was used to. But he was a sensible boy and had made up his mind to succeed in a legitimate fashion. Gradually he saved a few hundred dollars and, acting on the knowledge he had gained in his business, bought two or three shares in a security which quickly advanced in value and almost doubled his money. The next time as well fortune favored him, and he soon had a comfortable nest-egg—enough to warrant his feeling reasonably secure in the event of accident or sickness.

He had worked faithfully, had given great satisfaction to his employers, and presently had a clerical position in a prominent trust company offered to him. It seemed an advance. The salary was larger, even if absurdly small, and he gladly accepted the place.

Shortly after this he had his first experience in real finance. The president of the company sent for him—the reader will remember that this is a true story—and the boy entered his private office and came into the august presence of the magnate. This man is to-day what is commonly known as a "power" in Wall Street.

"My boy," said the president, "you have been doing very well. I have noticed the excellence of your work. I want to commend you."

"Thank you, sir," said John modestly, expecting to hear that his salary was to be raised.

"Yes," continued the great man. "And I want you to have an interest in the business."

The blood rushed to John's head and face. "Thank you very much," he gasped.

"I have allotted you five shares in the trust company," said the president. "If you take them up and carry them you will feel that you have a real connection with the house and it will net you a handsome return. Have you any money?"

It so happened that at this time John's savings were invested in a few bonds of an old and conservatively managed railroad. His heart fell. He didn't want to buy any bank stock.

"No," he answered. "My salary is small enough and I need it all. I don't save any money."

"Oh, well," said the magnate, "I will try and fix it up for you. I will arrange for a loan with the —— Bank on the stock. Remember, I'm doing this to help you. That is all. You may go back to your books."

Next day John was informed that he had bought five shares of —— Trust Company stock in the neighborhood of three hundred, and he signed a note for one thousand four hundred and twenty-five dollars, and indorsed the stock over to the bank from which the money had been borrowed for him. The stock almost immediately dropped over fifty points. John paid the interest on the note out of his salary, and the dividends, as fast as they were declared, went to extinguish the body of the loan. Some time afterward he learned that he had bought the stock from the magnate himself. He never received any benefit from it, for the stock was sold to cover the note, and John was obliged to make up the difference. He also discovered that ten or fifteen other employees had been given a similar opportunity by their generous employer at about the same time. John, in prison, says it was a scheme to keep fifty or a hundred shares where it could easily be controlled by the president, without risk to himself, in case of need. Of course, he may be wrong. At any rate, he feels bitterly now toward the big men who are at large while he is in jail.

John continued to keep up with the acquaintances formed during his years in the broker's office, many of whom had started little businesses of their own and had done well. Part of their stock-in-trade was to appear prosperous and they took John out to lunch, and told him what a fine fellow he was, and gave him sure tips. But John had grown "wise." He had had all the chances of that sort he wanted, and from a bigger man than any of them. He ate their lunches and invited them in return. Then he economized for a day or two to even up. He was not prosperous himself, but he did not accept favors without repaying them.

One thing he observed and noted carefully—every man he knew who had begun a brokerage business and kept sober, who attended to business and did not speculate, made money and plenty of it. He knew one young firm which cleared up fifteen thousand in commissions at the end of the second year. That looked good to him, and he knew, besides, that *he* was sober and attended to business. He made inquiries and learned that one could start in, if one were modest in one's pretensions, for two thousand five hundred dollars. That would pay office rent and keep things going until the commissions began to come in. He started to look around for some other young man who could put up the money in consideration of John's contributing the experience. But all the men he knew had experience without money.

Then by chance he met a young fellow of bright and agreeable personality whom we shall call Prescott. The latter was five or six years older than John, had had a large experience in brokerage houses in another city, and had come to New York to promote the interests of a certain copper company. John had progressed and was now assistant loan clerk of one of the biggest trust companies in the city, which also happened to be transfer agent for the copper company. Thus John had constantly to handle its certificates. Prescott said it was a wonderful thing—that some of the keenest men in the Street were in it, and, although it was a curb stock, strongly advised his new friend to buy all he could of it. He assured John that, although he was admittedly interested in booming the stock, he was confident that before long it would sell at four times its present quotation.

Meantime the stock, which had been listed at 2-1/4, began to go rapidly up. Word went around the trust company that it was a great purchase anywhere below 10, and John, as well as the other boys employed in the company, got together what money he could and began to buy it. It continued to go up—they had unconsciously assisted it in its ascent—and they bought more. John purchased seventy-five shares—all the way up to 8 and 9. One of his friends took eight hundred. Then it dropped out of sight. They hadn't time to get out, and John, in prison, has his yet. But he still had faith in Prescott, for he liked him and believed in his business capacity.

The stock "operation" over, Prescott began to prospect for something new, and suggested to John that they form a brokerage house under the latter's name. John was to be president at "a fixed salary." It sounded very grand. His duties at the trust company began to seem picayune. Moreover, his loss in copper had depressed him and he wanted to recoup, if he could. But how to get the two thousand five hundred dollars necessary to start in business? Prescott pleaded poverty, yet talked constantly of the ease with which a fortune might be made if they could only once "get in right." It was a period of increased dividends, of stock-jobbing operations of enormous magnitude, of "fifty-point movements," when the lucky purchaser of only a hundred shares of some inconspicuous railroad sometimes found that he could sell out next week with five thousand dollars' profit. The air seemed full of money. It appeared to rain banknotes and stock certificates.

In the "loan cage" at the trust company John handled daily millions in securities, a great part of which were negotiable. When almost everybody was so rich he wondered why any one remained poor. Two or three men of his own age gave up their jobs in other concerns and became traders, while another opened an office of his own. John was told that they had acted on "good information," had bought a few hundred shares of Union Pacific, and were now comfortably fixed. He would have been glad to buy, but copper had left him without anything to buy with.

One day Prescott took him out to lunch and confided to him that one of the big speculators had tipped him off to buy cotton, since there was going to be a failure in the crop. It was practically a sure thing. Two thousand dollars' margin would buy enough cotton to start them in business, even if the rise was only a very small one.

"Why don't you borrow a couple of bonds?" asked Prescott.

"Borrow from whom?" inquired John.

"Why, from some customer of the trust company."

"No one would lend them to me," answered John.

"Well, borrow them, anyhow. They would never know about it, and you could put them back as soon as we closed the account," suggested Prescott.

John was shocked, and said so.

"You are easy," said his comrade. "Don't you know that the trust companies do it themselves all the time? The presidents of the railroads use the holdings of their companies as collateral. Even the banks use their deposits for trading. Didn't old —— dump a lot of rotten stuff on you? Why don't you get even? Let me tell you something. Fully one-half of the men who are now successful financiers got their start by putting up as margin securities deposited with them. No one ever knew the difference, and now they are on their feet. If you took two bonds overnight you might put them back in the morning. Every one does it. It's part of the game."

"But suppose we lost?" asked John.

"You can't," said Prescott. "Cotton is sure to go up. It's throwing away the chance of your life."

John said he couldn't do such a thing, but when he returned to the office the cashier told him that a merger had been planned between their company and another—a larger one. John knew what that meant well enough—half the clerks would lose their positions. He was getting thirty-five dollars a week, had married a young wife, and, as he had told the magnate, he "needed it all." That night as he put the securities from the "loan cage" back in the vault the bonds burned his fingers. They were lying around loose, no good to anybody, and only two of them, overnight maybe, would make him independent of salaries and mergers—a free man and his own master.

The vault was in the basement just below the loan cage. It was some twenty feet long and ten wide. There were three tiers of boxes with double combination doors. In the extreme left-hand corner was the "loan box." Near it were two other boxes in which the securities of certain customers on deposit were kept. John had individual access to the loan box and the two others—one of which contained the collateral which secured loans that were practically permanent. He thus had within his control negotiable bonds of over a million dollars in value. The securities were in piles, strapped with rubber bands, and bore slips on which were written the names of the owners. Every morning John carried up all these piles to the loan cage—except the securities on deposit. At the end of the day he carried all back himself and tossed them into the boxes. When the interest coupons on the deposited bonds had to be cut he carried these, also, upstairs. At night the vault was secured by two doors, one with a combination lock and the other with a time lock. It was as safe as human ingenuity could make it. By day it had only a steel-wire gate which could be opened with a key. No attendant was stationed at the door. If John wanted to get in, all he had to do was to ask the person who had the key to open it. The reason John had the combination to these different boxes was in order to save the loan clerk the trouble of going downstairs to get the collateral himself.

Next day when John went out to lunch he put two bonds belonging to a customer in his pocket. He did not intend to steal them or even to borrow them. It was done almost automatically. His will seemed subjugated to the idea that they were to all intents and purposes *his* bonds to do as he liked with. He wanted the feeling of bonds-in-his-pocket. As he walked along the street to the restaurant, it seemed quite natural that they should be there. They were nearly as safe with him as lying around loose in the cage or chucked into a box in the vault. Prescott joined him, full of his new idea that cotton was going to jump overnight.

"If you only had a couple of bonds," he sighed.

Then somehow John's legs and arms grew weak. He seemed to disintegrate internally. He tried to pull himself together, but he had lost control of his muscles. He became a dual personality. His own John heard Prescott's John say quite naturally:

"I can let you have two bonds, but mind we get them back to-morrow, or anyhow the day after."

John's John felt the other John slip the two American Navigation 4s under the table and Prescott's fingers close upon them. Then came a period of hypnotic paralysis. The flywheel of his will-power hung on a dead centre. Almost instantly he became himself again.

"Give 'em back," he whispered hoarsely. "I didn't mean you should keep them," and he reached anxiously across the table. But Prescott was on his feet, half-way toward the door.

"Don't be a fool, Smith," he laughed. "What's the matter with you? It's a cinch. Go back and forget it." He shot out of the door and down the street.

John followed, dazed and trembling with horror at what he had done. He went back to the cage and remained the rest of the day in terror lest the broker who owned the two bonds should pay off his loan. But at the same time he had quickly made up his mind what he should do in that event. There was more than one loan secured by American Navigation 4s. He loosened a couple in one of the other piles. If the first broker came in he would take two bonds from one of these. But the broker did not come in.

That night John wandered the streets till nearly daylight. He saw himself arrested, ruined, in prison. Utterly fagged next morning, he called up Prescott on the telephone and begged him to return the bonds. Prescott laughed at his fears and assured him that everything was all right. Cotton was sure to go up. An hour later the broker who owned the bonds came in and took up his loan, and John removed two American Navigation 4s from another bundle and handed them to the loan clerk. Of course, the numbers on the bonds were not the same, but few persons would notice a little thing like that, even if they kept a record of it. They had the bonds—that was the main thing.

Once more John rushed to the 'phone, told Prescott what had occurred and besought him for the bonds.

"It's too late now," growled Prescott. "Cotton has gone down. I could only get one back at the most. We had better stand pat and get out on the next bulge."

John was by this time almost hysterical. The perspiration broke out on his forehead every now and then, and he shuddered as he counted his securities and entered up his figures. If cotton should go down some more! That was the hideous possibility. They would have to put up more margin, and then—!

Down in the vault where the depositors' bonds were kept were two piles of Overland 4s. One contained about two hundred and the other nearly six hundred bonds. The par value of these negotiable securities alone was nearly eight hundred thousand dollars. Twice a year John cut the coupons off of them. Each pile was marked with the owner's name. They were never called for, and it appeared that these customers intended to keep them there permanently. John, realizing that the chances of detection were smaller, removed two bonds from the pile of two hundred Overlands and substituted them with Prescott for the two Navigation 4s.

Then cotton went down with a slump. Prescott did not wait even to telephone. He came himself to the trust company and told John that they needed two more bonds for additional margin to protect their loan. But he said it was merely temporary, and that they had better even up by buying some more cotton. John went down into the vault and came back with four more Overland 4s bonds under his coat. He was in for it now and might as well be hung for a sheep as for a lamb. He was beginning to get used to the idea of being a thief. He was, to be sure, wretchedly unhappy, but he was experiencing the excitement of trying to dodge Fate until Fortune looked his way. Cotton still went down. It never occurred to him that Prescott perhaps had not bought all the cotton. Now that he is in prison he thinks maybe Prescott didn't. But he kept going down into the vault and bringing up more bonds, and, getting reckless, bought more cotton—quantities of it. In a month sixty bonds were gone from the pile of two hundred. John, a nervous wreck, almost laughed, grimly, at the joke of *his* being short sixty bonds!

At home they thought he was getting run down. His wife—! He was so kind and thoughtful that she had never been so happy. It made her fearful that he had some fatal disease and knew he was going to die. Up at the bank John made a separate bundle of sixty bonds out of the pile of six hundred so that he could substitute them for those first taken if the owner called for them. It was not likely that both owners would call for their bonds on the same day, so that he was practically safe until one or the other had withdrawn his deposit.

About this time the special accountants came around to make their annual investigation. It was apparently done in the regular and usual way. One examiner stood inside the vault and another outside, surrounded by four or five assistants. They "investigated" the loans. John brought them out in armfuls and the accountants checked them off and sent them back. When John brought out the one hundred and forty bonds left in the bundle of two hundred Overland 4s he placed on top of them the pile of sixty bonds taken from the other bundle of six hundred. Then he took them back, shifted over the sixty and brought out the bundle of six hundred Overland 4s made up in part of the same bonds. It was the easiest thing going. The experts simply counted the sixty bonds twice—and John had the sixty bonds (or Prescott had them) down the street. Later the same firm of "experts" certified to the presence of three hundred thousand dollars of missing bonds, counting the *same* bundle, not only twice, but five and six times! You see, Prescott's John had grown wise in his generation.

After that he felt reasonably secure. It did seem almost unbelievable that such a situation could exist, but it was, nevertheless, a fact that it did. He expected momentarily that his theft would be detected and that he would be thrown into prison, and the fear of the actual arrest, the moment of public ignominy, the shock and agony of his wife and family, were what drove him sleepless into the streets, and every evening to the theatres to try to forget what must inevitably come; but the fact that he had "gone wrong," that he was a thief, that he had betrayed his trust, had lost its edge. He now thought no more of shoving a package of bonds into his overcoat pocket than he did of taking that garment down from its peg behind the door. He knew from inquiry that men who stole a few hundred dollars, and were caught, usually got as long a term as those who stole thousands. If he stole one bond he was just as likely to get ten years in State's prison as if he stole fifty—so he stole fifty, and when they were wiped out he stole fifty more—and, well, if the reader is interested he will learn before the end of the story just what John *did* steal.

Somehow, Prescott's speculations never succeeded. Occasionally they would make a good turn and get a few bonds back, but the next week there would be a new fiasco, and John would have to visit the Overland 4s again. That performance of the accountants had given him a huge contempt for bankers and banking. He knew that if he wanted to he could grab up a million any day and walk off with it, but he didn't want to. All he desired now was to get back to where he was before. All the speculation was in the hands of Prescott, and Prescott never seemed worried in the least. He called on John almost daily for what extra bonds were needed as additional collateral, and John took his word absolutely as to the result of the transactions. He could not do otherwise, for one word from Prescott would have ruined him.

Before long the pile of two hundred Overland 4s was gone. So was a large quantity of other securities, for John and Prescott had dropped cotton and gone plunging into the stock market. Here, however, they had no better success than before. Of course, a difficulty arose when the interest on the Overland 4s came due. The coupons had to be cut by some one in the bank, and although John usually cut them he did not always do so. Sometimes the loan clerk himself would take a hand, and call for a particular lot of bonds. John, however, was now fertile in devices. The owner of the larger pile of six hundred bonds usually wrote to have his coupons cut about the twenty-seventh of April. John would make up a collection of six hundred bonds of the same sort, carry them up and cut the coupons in the loan cage. The other man generally sent in a draft for his interest on the second or third of May. But now the bonds were away, scattered all over the Street. So John started a new operation to get the bonds back and straighten out the coupon tangle. He substituted with the brokers an equal number of bonds of other companies, the interest upon which was not yet due. There was a large block of Electric 5s and Cumberland 4s which served his purpose admirably, and thus he kept up with the game. When the coupons became due on the latter he carried back the first. It kept him and Prescott busy most of the time juggling securities—at least John knew *he* was kept busy, and Prescott claimed to be equally so.

There were many loans of brokers and others all secured by the same sort of collateral. Most of these John appropriated. When it was necessary to check off the loans, John, having retained enough of the same kind of bonds to cover the largest loan, would bring up the same bundle time after time with a different name upon it. If one of the customers wanted to pay off a loan and his bonds were gone he would be given some one else's collateral. Apparently the only thing that was necessary was to have enough of each kind of security on hand to cover the largest loan on the books at any given time.

Once, when the examiners were at work on the vault, John had to make up one hundred thousand dollars in Overland 4s or 5s from the different small loans in the loan vault and put them in a package in the deposit vault in order to make it appear that certain depositors' bonds were all there.

The most extraordinary performance of all was when, upon one of the annual examinations, John covered the absence of over fifty bonds in the collateral covering a certain loan by merely shoving the balance of the securities into the back of the vault, so that it was not examined at all. He had taken these bonds to substitute for others in different brokers' offices, and it so happened that there were no similar securities in the building; thus the deficiency could not be covered up even by John's expert sleight of hand. Of course, if there had been other bonds of the same kind in another vault it would have been a simple matter to substitute them. But there were not. So John pushed the remaining one hundred and fifty bonds into a dark corner of the vault and awaited the discovery with throbbing pulses. Yet, strange to relate, these watchdogs of finance, did not see the bonds which John had hidden, and did not discover that anything was wrong, since, for purposes of its own, the bank had neglected to make any record of the loan in question. It would really have been safer for John if he had taken the whole pile, but then he did not know that the accountants were going to do their business in any such crazy fashion. The whole thing came to seem a sort of joke to John. He never took any bonds for his own personal use. He gave everything to Prescott, and he rarely, if ever, saw Prescott except to hand him securities.

One day Prescott walked right into the bank itself and John gave him one hundred and sixty-five bonds, which he stuffed under his overcoat and carried away. Remember that this is a *fact*.

The thing, which began in August, 1905, dragged over through the following year and on into 1907. John weathered two examinations by the accountants, the last being in October, 1906, when they certified that the company was absolutely "O.K." and everything intact. On that particular day John had over three hundred thousand dollars in Overland 4s and 5s scattered over the Street.

In the first six months they lost one hundred thousand dollars in cotton. Then they played both sides of the market in stocks and got badly bitten as bears in the temporary bull market in the autumn of 1906, selling Union Pacific at 165, which afterward went to 190, Northern Pacific at 185, which went to 200, etc., etc. Then they shifted their position, became bulls and went long of stock just at the beginning of the present slump. They bought Reading at 118, American Smelters at 126, Pennsylvania at 130, Union at 145, and Northern Pacific at 180. At one time John had five hundred and fifty thousand dollars in bonds out of the vaults.

The thing might have been going on still had it not been for the fact that the anticipated merger between John's company and another was put through and a new vault in a new building prepared to receive the securities. Of course, on such an occasion a complete examination would be made of all the securities and there would be practically no chance to deceive the accountants. Moreover, a part of the securities had actually been moved when the worst slump came and they needed more. It was obvious that the jig was up. A few more days and John knew that the gyves would be upon his wrists. Prescott and he took an account of the stock they had lost and went into committee on ways and means. Neither had any desire to run away. Wall Street was the breath of life to them. Prescott said that the best thing to do was to take enough more to "stand off" the company. He cited a case in Boston, where a clerk who was badly "in" was advised by his lawyer to take a hundred and twenty-five thousand dollars more. Then the lawyer dickered with the bank and brought it to terms. The lawyer got twenty-five thousand dollars, the bank got the rest, and the thief was let go. Prescott said they ought to get away with enough more to make the bank's loss a million. He thought *that* would make them see what was the wise thing to do. Prescott also said he would try to get a lawyer who could bring some pressure to bear on the officials of the company. It would be a rather unpleasant situation to have brought to the attention of the State Superintendent of Banking. John agreed to get the additional securities and turn them over to Prescott. Unfortunately, almost everything had by this time been moved into the new vault, and all John could get was a stock certificate for fifteen hundred railroad shares, standing in his own name, and seventy-five thousand dollars in notes. These he gave to Prescott, thus increasing the amount stolen from the bank without discovery to between six and seven hundred thousand dollars. This was on the day before the actuaries were to make their investigation. Knowing that his arrest was now only a question of time, John, about eleven o'clock on the following morning, left the trust company for the last time. He was in telephonic communication with Prescott, who, in turn, was in touch with their lawyer. Unfortunately, the president of the company had gone out of town over Sunday, so that again their plans went awry.

For nearly two years John had not known an hour devoid of haunting fear. From a cheerful and contented youth he had become despondent, taciturn and nervous. He was the same affectionate husband and attentive son as before, and his general characteristics remained precisely the same. He was scrupulous to a penny in every other department of his life, and undoubtedly would have felt the same pricks of conscience had he been guilty of any other act of dishonesty. The affair at the bank was a thing apart. The embezzler of six hundred thousand dollars was not John at all, but a separate personality wearing John's clothes and bearing his name. He perceived clearly the enormity of his offense, but, because he was the same John in every other respect, he had a feeling that somehow the fact that *he* had done the thing was purely fortuitous—in other words, that the bonds had to be taken, were going to be taken anyway, and that Fate had simply elected him to take them. Surely he had not wanted the bonds—had had no intention of stealing half a million dollars, and, in short, was not the kind of a man who would steal half a million dollars. Each night he tossed, sleepless, till the light stole in through the shutters. At every corner on his way uptown he glanced over his shoulder behind him. The front doorbell never rang that his muscles did not become rigid and his heart almost stop beating. If he went to a theatre or upon an excursion he passed the time wondering if the next day he would still be a free man. In short, he paid in full in physical misery and mental anxiety and wretchedness for the real moral obliquity of his crime. The knowledge of this maddened him for what was coming. Yet he realized that he had stolen half a million dollars, and that justice demanded that he should be punished for it.

After leaving the bank John called up Prescott and learned that the plan to adjust matters with the president had miscarried by reason of the latter's absence. The two then met in a saloon, and here it was arranged that John should call up the loan clerk and tell him that something would be found to be wrong at the bank, but that nothing had better be said about it until the following Monday morning, when the president would return. The loan clerk, however, refused to talk with him and hung up the receiver. John had nowhere to go, for he dared not return home, and spent the afternoon until six o'clock riding in street cars and sitting in saloons. At that hour he again communicated with Prescott, who said that he had secured rooms for him and his wife at a certain hotel, where they might stay until matters could be fixed up. John arranged to meet his wife at Forty-second Street with Prescott and conduct her to the hotel. As Fate decreed, the loan clerk came out of the subway at precisely the same time, saw them together and followed them. Meantime a hurry call had been sent for the president, who had returned to the city. John, fully aware that the end had come, went to bed at the hotel, and, for the first time since the day he had taken the bonds two years before, slept soundly. At three the next morning there came a knock at the door. His wife awakened him and John opened it. As he did so a policeman forced his way in, and the loan clerk, who stood in the corridor just behind him, exclaimed theatrically, "Officer, there is your man!"

John is now in prison, serving out the sentence which the court believed it necessary to inflict upon him as a warning to others. Prescott is also serving a term at hard labor—a sentence somewhat longer than John's. The trust company took up their accounts, paid the losses of the luckless pair, and, owing to a rise in prices which came too late to benefit the latter, escaped with the comparatively trifling loss of a little over one hundred thousand dollars. At once every banking house and trust company upon the Street looked to its system of checks upon the honesty of its employees, and took precautions which should have been taken long before. The story was a nine days' wonder. Then Union Pacific dropped twenty points more, the tide of finance closed over the heads of John and Prescott, and they were forgotten.

Had the company, instead of putting itself at the mercy of a thirty-five-dollar-a-week clerk, placed double combinations on the loan and deposit vaults, and employed two men, one to act as a check upon the other, to handle its securities, or had it merely adopted the even simpler expedient of requiring an officer of the company to be present when any securities were to be removed from the vaults, John would probably not now be in jail. It would seem that it would not be a difficult or complicated matter to employ a doorkeeper, who did not have access himself, to stand at the door of the vault and check off all securities removed therefrom or returned thereto. An officer of the bank should personally see that the loans earned up to the cage in the morning were properly returned to the vaults at night and secured with a time lock.

Such a precaution would not cost the Stockholders a tenth of one per cent. in dividends.

It is a trite saying that an ounce of prevention is worth a pound of cure. But this is as true, in the case of financial institutions at least, from the point of view of the employe as of the company. It is an ingenious expedient to insure one's self with a "fidelity corporation" against the possible defalcations of one's servants, and doubtless certain risks can only be covered in some such fashion. These methods are eminently proper so far as they go, but they, unfortunately, do not serve the public purpose of protecting the weak from undue and unnecessary temptation. Banks and trust companies are prone to rely on the fact that most peculations are easily detected and severely punished, but the public interest demands that all business, State, municipal and private, should be so conducted that dishonesty may not only be punished, but prevented.

A builder who "took a chance" on the strength of a girder would have small credit in his profession. A good bridge is one which will bear the strain—not only of the pedestrian, but of the elephant. A deluge or an earthquake may occur and the bridge may tumble, but next time it is built stronger and better. Thus science progresses and the public interest is subserved. A driver who overloads his beast is regarded as a fool or a brute. Perhaps such names are too harsh for those who overload the moral backbone of an inexperienced subordinate. Surely the fault is not all on one side. While there are no formulas to calculate the resiliency of human character, we may demand the same prudence on the part of the officers of financial institutions as we do from nursemaids, lumbermen and manufacturers of explosives. Though we may have confidence in the rectitude of our fellows, we have no right to ignore the limitations and weaknesses of mankind. It would not outrage the principles of justice if one who placed needless and disproportionate strain upon the morals of another were himself regarded as an accessory to the crime.

VII
The "Duc de Nevers"

"And God gives to every manThe virtue, temper, understanding, taste,That lifts him into life, and lets him fallJust in the niche he was ordained to fill."—"The Task"—COWPER.

One morning there lay on my desk a note finely written in pencil and dated:

TOMBS PRISON.

MONSIEUR:

Will you be so gracious as to extend to the undersigned the courtesy of a private interview in your office? I have a communication of the highest importance to make to you.

Respectfully,

CHARLES JULIUS FRANCIS DE NEVERS.

Across the street in the courtyard the prisoners were taking their daily exercise. Two by two they marched slowly around the enclosure in the centre of which a small bed of geraniums struggled bravely in mortal combat with the dust and grime of Centre Street. Some of the prisoners walked with heads erect and shoulders thrown back, others slouched along with their arms dangling and their chins resting upon their chests. When one of them failed to keep up with the rest, a keeper, who stood in the shade by a bit of ivy in a corner of the wall, got after him. Somehow the note on the desk did not seem to fit any one of the gentry whom I could see so distinctly from my window. The name, too, did not have the customary Tombs sound—De Nevers? *De Nevaire*—I repeated it slowly to myself with varying accent. It seemed as though I had known the name before. It carried with it a suggestion of the novels of Stanley J. Weyman, of books on old towns and the châteaux and cathedrals of France. I wondered who the devil Charles Julius Francis de Nevers could be.

Of course, if one answered all the letters one gets from the Tombs it would keep a secretary busy most of the working hours of the day, and if one acceded to all the various requests the prisoners make to interview them personally or to see their fathers, mothers, sisters, brothers, sweethearts and wives, a prosecutor might as well run an intelligence office and be done with it. But as I re-read the note I began to have a sneaking feeling of curiosity to see what Charles Julius Francis de Nevers looked like, so I departed from the usual rule of my office, rang for a messenger and directed him to ascertain the full name of the prisoner from whom the note had come, the crime with which he was charged, and the date of his incarceration, also to supply me at once with copies of the indictment and the complaint; then I instructed him to have De Nevers brought over as soon as he could be got into shape.

I had almost forgotten that I was expecting a visitor when, a couple of hours later, an undersized deputy-sheriff entered my office and reported that he had a prisoner in his custody for whom I had sent to the Tombs. Glancing up from my desk I saw standing behind his keeper a tall and distinguished-looking man in fashionably cut garments, whose well shaped head and narrow face, thin aquiline nose, and carefully trimmed pointed beard seemed to bespeak somewhat different antecedents from those of the ordinary occupant of a cell in the City Prison. I should have instinctively risen from my chair and offered my aristocratic looking visitor a chair had not the keeper unconsciously brought me to a realization of my true position by remarking:

"Say, Counsellor, I guess while you're talking to his nibs I'll step out into the hall and take a smoke."

"Certainly," said I, glad to be rid of him, "I will be responsible for the—er—prisoner."

Then, as the keeper hesitated in putting his suggestion into execution, I reached into the upper right-hand drawer of my desk, produced two of what are commonly known in the parlance of the Criminal Courts Building as "cigars" and handed them to him.

"Well," said I, after the keeper had departed closing the door behind him and leaving the visitor standing in the middle of the office, "I have sent for you as you requested and shall be glad to hear anything you have to say. Of course any communication which you may see fit to make to me is voluntary and, in the event for your trial for—er—any crime with which you may be charged, may be used against you." I had a certain feeling of embarrassment in making this customary declaration since the whole idea of this person being a criminal was so incongruous as to put a heavy strain on one's credulity. However, I recalled that a certain distinguished Englishman of letters has declared "that there is no essential incongruity between crime and culture." He acknowledged my remark with a slight smile of half-amused deprecation and with a courteous bow took the seat to which I motioned him.

"I wish to thank you," he said in excellent English marked by the slightest possible suggestion of a foreign accent, "for your exceeding courtesy in responding so quickly to my request. I am aware," he added, "that it is unusual for prisoners to seek interviews with the—what shall I say—*juge d'instruction*, as we call him, but," he added with a smile, "I think you will find that mine is an unusual affair."

I had already begun to think so, and reaching to the upper drawer on the left-hand side of my desk, I produced from the box reserved for judges, prominent members of the bar, borough presidents, commissioners of departments and distinguished foreigners, a Havana of the variety known in our purlieus as a "*good* cigar," and tendered the same to him.

"Ah," he said, "many thanks, *merci, non*, I do not smoke the cigar. M'sieu' perhaps has a cigarette? M'sieu' will pardon me if I say that this is the first act of kindness which has been accorded to me since my incarceration three weeks ago."

Somewhere I found a box of cigarettes, one of which he removed, gracefully holding it between fingers which I noticed were singularly white and delicate, and lighting it with the air of a diplomat at an international conference.

"You can hardly appreciate," he ventured, "the humiliation to which I, an officer and a gentleman of France, have been subjected."

I lighted the cigar which he had declined and with mingled feelings of embarrassment, distrust and curiosity inquired if his name was Charles Julius Francis de Nevers. I wish it were possible to describe the precise look which flashed across his face as he answered my question.

"That is my name," he said, "or at least rather, I am Charles Julius Francis, and I am of Nevers. May I speak confidentially? Were my family to be aware of my present situation they would never recover from the humiliation and disgrace connected with it."

"Certainly," said I, "anything which you may tell me which you wish to be kept confidential I will treat as such, provided, of course, that what you tell me is the truth."

"You shall hear nothing else," he replied. Then leaning back in his chair he said simply and with great dignity, "I am by direct inheritance today the Duc de Nevers, my father, the last duke, having died in the month of February, 1905."

Any such announcement would ordinarily have filled me with amusement, but that the gentleman sitting before me should declare himself to be a duke or even a prince seemed entirely natural.

"Indeed!" said I, unable to think of any more appropriate remark.

"Yes," said De Nevers, "and M'sieu' is naturally surprised that one of my distinguished position should be now a tenant of an American jail. But if M'sieu' will do me the honor of listening for a few moments I will explain my present extraordinary predicament. I am Charles Julius François, eldest son of the late Oscar Odon, Duc de Nevers, Grand Commander of the Legion of Honor, and Knight of the Garter. I was born in Paris in the year 1860 at 148 Rue Champs Elysée; my mother, the dowager duchess, is now residing at the Château de Nevers in the Province of Nievre in France. My sister Jeanne married Prince Henry of Aremberg, and now lives in Brussells at the Palais d'Aremberg, situated at the corner of the Rue de Regence near the Palais de Justice. My sister Louise, the Countess of Kilkenny, is living in Ireland. My sister Camille married the Marquis of Londonderry and is residing in London at the present time. My sister Evelyn married the Earl of Dudley and is living in Dublin. I have one other sister, Marie, who is with my mother. My brother, Count André de Nevers is at present Naval Attaché at Berlin. My brother Fernand is an officer of artillery stationed in Madagascar, and my youngest brother Marcel is also an officer of artillery attached to the 8th Regiment in Nancy. I make this statement by way of introduction in order that you may understand fully my situation. During my childhood I had an English tutor in Paris, and when I reached the age of ten years I was sent by my father to the College Louis le Grand where I took the course of Science and Letters and graduated from the Lycée with the degree of Bachelor on the 5th of August, 1877. Having passed my examination for the Polytechnic I remained there two years, and on my graduation received a commission as Sous-Lieutenant of Engineers, and immediately entered the Application School at Fontainebleau, where I was graduated in 1881 as Lieutenant of Engineers and assigned to the First Regiment of Engineers at Versailles—"

De Nevers paused and exhaled the cigarette smoke.

"M'sieu' will pardon me if I go into detail for only in that way will he be convinced of the accuracy of what I am telling him."

"Pray, go on," said I. "If what you tell me is true your case is extraordinary indeed."

"My first act of service," continued De Nevers, "was on the 10th of August when I was sent to Tonkin. I will not trouble you with the details of my voyage on the transport to China, but will simply state that I was wounded in the engagement at Yung Chuang on the 7th of November of the same year and had the distinction of receiving the Cross of the Legion of Honor therefor. I was immediately furloughed back to France, where I entered the Superior School of War and took my Staff Major brevet. At the same time I seized the opportunity to follow the course of the Sorbonne and secured the additional degree of Doctor of Science. I had received an excellent education in my youth and always had a taste for study, which I have taken pains to pursue in whatever part of the world I happened to be stationed. As a result I am able to converse with considerable fluency in English, as perhaps you have already observed, as well as in Spanish, Italian, German, Russian, Arabic, and, to a considerable extent, in Japanese.

"In 1883 I was sent to Berlin as Military Attaché, but was subsequently recalled because I had violated the rules of international etiquette by fighting three duels with German officers. The Ambassador at this time was Charles de Courcel. You will understand that there was no disgrace connected with my recall, but the necessity of defending my honor was incompatible with the rules of the service, and after fifteen months in Berlin I was remanded to Versailles with the rank of First Lieutenant, under Colonel Quinivet. Here I pursued my studies and was then ordered to the Soudan, whence, after being wounded, I was sent to Senegal. Here I acted as Governor of the City of St. Louis. As you are doubtless aware, the climate of Senegal is exceedingly unhealthy. I fell ill with a fever and was obliged to return to France where I was assigned to the office of the General Staff Major in Paris. At the opening of the war with Dahomey in 1892, I was sent in command of the Engineers of the Corps Expeditional, and on the 17th of November of that year was severely wounded at Dakar in Dahomey, having received a spear cut through the lungs. On this occasion I had the distinction of being promoted as Major of Engineers and was created an Officer of the Legion of Honor on the battle field. The wound in my lungs was of such a serious character that Colonel Dodds sent me back once more to France on furlough, and President Carnot was kind enough to give me his personal commendation for my services.

"I was now thirty-three years old and had already attained high rank in my profession. I had had opportunity to pursue studies in chemistry, medicine and science, and my only interest was in the service of my country and in qualifying myself for my future duties. My life up to that time had been uniformly happy; I was the eldest son and beloved both of my father and mother. My social position gave me the entrée to the best of society wherever I happened to be. As yet, however, I had never been in love. At this time occurred the affair which in a measure changed my career. The wound in my lungs was slow in healing, and at the earnest invitation of my sister, Lady Londonderry, I went to London. At that time she was living in Belgravia Square. It was here I met my first wife."

De Nevers paused. The cigarette had gone out. For the first time he seemed to lose perfect control of himself. I busied myself with some papers until he should have regained his self possession.

"You will understand," he said in a few moments, "these things are not governed by law and statute. The woman with whom I fell in love and who was in every respect the equal in intellectual attainments, beauty and charm of manner of my own people, was the nursery governess in my sister's household. She returned my affection and agreed to marry me. The proposed marriage excited the utmost antipathy on the part of my family; my fiancée was dismissed from my sister's household, and I returned to Paris with the intention of endeavoring by every means in my power to induce my father to permit me to wed the woman I loved. It is doubtless difficult for M'sieu' to appreciate the position of a French officer. In America—Ah—America is free, one can marry the woman one loves, but in France no officer can marry without the consent of the Minister of War and of the President of the Republic; and more than that he cannot marry unless his intended wife possesses a dowry of at least fifty thousand francs which must be deposited with the Minister of War for investment."

"In spite of the fact that I enjoyed the confidence and friendship of President Carnot the latter, at my father's request, refused me permission to marry. There was no choice left for me but to resign my commission, and this I did. I returned to England and was married at St. Thomas's Church, London, on the 21st of June, 1893.

"My education as an engineer had been of the most highly technical and thorough character, and I had every reason to believe that in America I could earn a comfortable living. My wife and I, therefore, sailed for America immediately after our marriage. I first secured a position in some iron works in South Boston, and for a time lived happily. A boy, Oscar, named after my father, was born to us while we were living in the town of Winchester near Boston. Another son was born a year later in the same place, and still a third in Pittsburgh, where I had gone to assume the position of general foreman of the Homestead Steel Works and assistant master mechanic of the Carnegie Steel Company. I rapidly secured the confidence of my employers and was sent upon several occasions to study new processes in different parts of the country. During one of my vacations we returned to England and visited my wife's people, who lived in Manchester; here she died on the 17th of June, 1901."

De Nevers paused again and it was some moments before he continued.

"After the death of my wife my father expressed himself as ready for a reconciliation, but although this took place I had not the heart to remain in France. I liked America and had attained distinction in my profession. I therefore expressed my intention of returning to continue my career as an engineer, but at the earnest solicitation of my father, left my three children with my parents. They are now living at the château of my mother at Nievre.

"I was sent to Chicago to study a new blast furnace, and two years later, when Mr. Schwab organized the Russo-American Company at Mariopool, South Siberia, he offered me the position of general manager, which I accepted. Here I remained until November, 1904, when all the American engineers were arrested and imprisoned on the order of General Kozoubsky of the Russian Engineers, who at the same time shot and murdered my assistant, Thomas D. McDonald, for refusing to allow him to remove pig iron from the storehouse without giving a receipt for it. Ambassador McCormick secured our immediate release, and we returned to the States. M'sieu' has no idea of the power of these Russian officers. The murder of my assistant was of the most brutal character. Kozoubsky came to my office and demanded the iron, but having secured it, refused to sign the receipt which McDonald presented to him. McDonald said: 'You shall not remove the iron if you do not sign the receipt.' As he spoke the words the General drew his revolver and shot him down like a dog.

"I returned to America in January, 1905, and have since then been doing work as a consulting engineer. Last January I visited my parents in Paris at their home at 148 Champs Elysée. You have doubtless seen the mansion with its two gates and black railing of decorative iron. I had no sooner returned to America than I received a cable announcing the death of my father."

De Nevers removed from his breast pocket a bundle of carefully folded papers from which he produced a sheet of heavy stationery with a deep border of mourning and a large black cross at the top, of which the following is a copy:

MM. Her Grace the Duchess Dowager of Nevers; his Grace the Duke Charles J. F. of Nevers and his children Oscar, Hilda and John; their Highnesses the Prince and Princess Henry of Aremberg; Captain the Count André of Nevers; Captain the Count Fernand of Nevers; the Earl and Countess of Kilkenny; the Marquis and Marchioness of Londonderry; the Earl and Countess of Dudley; the Countess Marie of Nevers; Lieutenant the Count Marcel of Nevers have the sorrow to announce the subite death at the family seat at Nevers (France), of His Grace Oscar Odon, Duke of Nevers, Grand Commander of the Legion of Honor, Knight of the Garter. Their husband, father, grandfather and uncle beloved.

Masonic burial shall take place at Nevers on Tuesday, February 21, 1905.

New York, February 20, 1905.

U. S. A.

The announcement was carefully engraved and was of an expensive character, and I read it with considerable interest.

"Does M'sieu' care to see the photographs of my family? Here," producing a photograph of a gentleman and lady and a group of children, "is my wife with the three children, taken in London just before she died."

Another group, bearing the trade-mark of a Parisian photographer, exhibited a distinguished looking man surrounded by a group of many children of varying ages.

"These," said De Nevers, "are my father and my brothers and sisters."

Then came photographs of Lady Londonderry and the Earl and Countess of Dudley. My interest in my visitor's story had for the moment completely driven from my mind the real object of the interview, which, ostensibly, was to explain the reason for his incarceration. His straightforward narrative carried absolute conviction with it; that he was the legitimate Duc de Nevers I accepted without hesitation; that he was a man of education, culture and many accomplishments, was self evident.

"You have had an extraordinary career," I ventured.

"Yes," he replied, "it has been a life of action and I may say of suffering. Permit me to show you the certificate of my general that what I have told you is accurate."

And De Nevers unfolded from his pocket a document, bearing a seal of the French Ministry of War, which read as follows:

REPUBLIQUE FRANÇAISE

MINISTERE DE LA GUERRE

CABINET DU MINISTERE

No. 195

PARIS, *October 24, 1901.*

To Whom It May Concern:

I, George André, General of Division of Engineers, Minister of War of the French Republic, certify that the Lieutenant Colonel Charles Jules Comte François de Nevers, is connected with the French Army, since the 10th day of September, 1877, and that the following is a true copy of his record:

Born in Paris the 10th of June, 1859.

Graduated, Bachelor of Sciences and of Letters, from the Lycée, Louis le Grand, the 5th of August, 1877.

Received first as Chief of Promotion of the National Polytechnic School of France, the 10th of September, 1877.

Graduated with the greatest distinction from the above school the 1st of September, 1879.

Entered at the Application School of Military Engineers at Fontainebleau as Second Lieutenant, Chief of Promotion the 15th of September, 1879.

Graduated as Lieutenant of Engineers with great distinction, the 1st of August, 1881, and sent to the First Regiment of Engineers at Versailles.

Sent to Tonkin the 1st day of August, 1881.

Wounded at Yung Chuang (Tonkin) the 7th of November, 1881.

Inscribed on the Golden Book of the French Army the 10th of November, 1881.

Made Knight of the Legion of Honor the 10th of November, 1881.

Wounded at Suai Sing the 4th of January, 1882.

Sent to Switzerland in Mission where he was graduated at the Zurich Polytechnic University as Mechanical Engineer, 1884.

Sent the 2nd of January, 1885, to Soudan.

Wounded there twice.

Made Captain of Engineers the 3rd of June, 1885.

Called back to France the 6th of September, 1885, sent in Mission in Belgium, where he was graduated as Electrical Engineer from the Montefiore University at Liege. Made officer of Academy.

Sent in Gabon, the 2nd of May, 1887. Wounded twice. Constructed there the Military Railroad.

Sent to Senegal as Commander the 6th of July, 1888, to organize administration. Wounded once.

Called back and sent to Germany the 7th of December, 1889.

Called back from Germany and assigned to the Creusot as Assistant Chief Engineer.

Sent to Dahomey, the 1st of January, 1891. Wounded the 19th of November, 1892, at Dahomey. Made Major of Engineers on the battle field. Made Officer of the Legion of Honor, on the battle field.

By special decision of the Senate and the Chamber of Representatives the name of Commandant Charles Jules Comte François de Nevers is embroidered the 21st of November, on the flag of the Regiment of Engineers.

Called back and sent to Algeria, the 3rd of January, 1893.

Made Ordinance of the President Carnot, the 5th of February, 1893.

Sent to the Creusot the 1st of July, 1893, as director.

Sent to Madagascar the 2nd of April, 1894, in command of the Engineers.

Wounded the 12th of July, 1894, at Majungua.

Made Lieutenant Colonel of Engineers the 12th of July, 1894, on the battle field.

Proposed as Commander of the Legion of Honor on the same date.

Called back and sent as Ordinance Officer of the General in Chief in Command in Algeria, the 4th of March, 1896.

Sent to America in special mission to the Klondike the 7th of July, 1897.

Put on disponsibility *Hors Cadre* on his demand the 1st of November, 1897.

Made Honorary Member of the National Defences. Commissioned the 28th of January, 1898.

Made Honorary Member of the Commission on Railroads, Canals, and Harbors, the 7th of July, 1899.

Made Honorary Member of the Commission on Bridges and Highways the 14th of July, 1900.

Made Corresponding Member of the Academy of Sciences, the 14th of July, 1901.

Made Commander of the Legion of Honor the 22nd of October, 1901.

I will say further that the Lieutenant Colonel Charles Jules Comte François de Nevers, is regarded as one of our best and most loyal officers, that he has the good will and best wishes of the government and of all his fellow officers, and is considered by everybody as a great worker and a thoroughly honest man. I personally will be pleased to do anything in my power to help him in any business he may undertake, and can recommend him to everybody as a responsible and trustworthy Engineer, knowing him for the last twenty-four years.

GEO. ANDRÉ,
Minister of War.
[Seal]

The document seemed in substance merely a repetition of what De Nevers had already told me, and I handed it back to him satisfied of its correctness. But public business is public business, and if the Duc de Nevers had anything to communicate to me in my official character it was time for him to do so.

"Well, Duke," said I, not knowing very well how otherwise to address him, "do you desire to communicate anything to me in connection with your present detention in the Tombs?"

"Ah," he said with a gesture of deprecation, "I can hardly understand that myself. Perhaps M'sieu' has the papers? Ah, yes, I see they are on his desk. M'sieu' will observe that I am accused of the crime of—what is it called in English? Ah, yes, perjury, but I assure M'sieu' that it is entirely a mistake."

I picked up the indictment and found that the Grand Jury of the County of New York accused one Charles de Nevers of the crime of perjury committed as follows:

That one William Douglas having been arrested by William W. Crawford, a member of the Police force of the City of New York, upon the charge of having violated the motor vehicle law of the State of New York [ordinance against speeding] he, the said Charles de Nevers, had then and there offered himself to go bail for the said Douglas, and did sign a certain written undertaking called a bond for the appearance of the said Douglas before the Magistrate, wherein he swore that he owned a certain house and lot situate at 122 West 117th Street, in the County of New York, which was free and clear of all incumbrances and of the value of not less than twenty thousand dollars,

Whereas in truth and in fact he the said Charles de Nevers did not own the said house and lot which did not then and there stand in the name of him the said Charles de Nevers, but was the property of one Helen M. Bent, and so recorded in the Registry of Deeds.

Which, said the grand jury, Charles de Nevers then and there well knew. And so they accused him of feloniously, knowingly, wilfully, corruptly, and falsely committing the crime of perjury against the form of the statute in such cases made and provided, and against the peace of the People of the State of New York and their dignity.

And this they did over the signature of William Travers Jerome, District Attorney.

"How did this happen?" I inquired, hardly believing my senses. "Was it a fact that you made this false statement to the Police for the purpose of securing bail for Mr. Douglas?"

De Nevers leaned forward and was about to answer when a messenger entered the room and stated that I was wanted in the court.

"Another time, if M'sieu' will permit me," said he. "I have much to thank you for. If M'sieu' will give me another hearing it shall be my pleasure to explain fully."

I rose and summoned the keeper. De Nevers bowed and offered his hand, which I took.

"I have much to thank you for!" he repeated.

As I hurried out of the room I encountered the keeper outside the door.

"Say, Counsellor, what sort of a 'con' was he throwin' into you?" he inquired with a wink.

De Nevers was well inside my office, looking drearily out of my window towards the courtyard in the Tombs where his fellows were still pursuing their weary march.

"What do you mean?" I asked.

"Why, who did his nibs tell you he was?"

"The Duc de Nevers," I replied.

"Say," said O'Toole, "you don't mean you swallowed that, do you? Do you know what the feller did? Why, one afternoon when a swell guy and his girl were out in their gas wagon a mounted cop in the park pulls them in and takes them over to the 57th Street Court. Well, just as me friend is taking them into the house along walks this Charley Nevers wid his tall silk hat and pearl handle cane, wid a flower in his buttonhole, and his black coat tails dangling around his heels, just like Boni de Castellane, and says he, 'Officer,' says he, 'may I inquire what for you're apprehending this gentleman and lady?' says he. With that me friend hands him out some strong language for buttin' in, and Charley is so much shocked at the insult to himself and the lady that he steps in before the Sergeant and offers to go bond for Douglas, just to go the cop one better, givin' the Sergeant the same line of drip that he has been handin' out to us in the Tombs, about his bein' the son of Oscar, the Duc de Nevers, and related to all the crowned heads in Europe. Then he ups and signs the bail bond for a house and lot that he has never seen in his life. And here he is up agin it. An' it's a good stiff one His Honor will be handin' out to him to my way of thinkin', for these high fallutin' foreigners has got to be put a stop to, and Charley Nevers is a good one to begin on."

"I think you're wrong, O'Toole," said I. "But we can tell better later on."

All that day my thoughts kept reverting to the Duc de Nevers. One thing was more than certain and that was that of all the various personages whom I had met during my journey through the world none was more fitted to be a duke than he. I was obliged to confess that during my hour's interview I had felt myself to be in the company of a superior being, one of different clay from that of which I was composed, a man of better brain, and better education, vastly more rounded and experienced, a cultivated citizen of the world, who would be at home in any company no matter how distinguished and who would rise to any emergency. As I ate my dinner at the club the name De Nevers played mistily in the recesses of my memory. *De Nevers!* Surely there was something historic about it, some flavor of the days of kings and courtiers. Smoking my cigar in the library I fell into a reverie in which the Tombs, with its towers and grated windows, figured as a gray château of old Tourraine, and Charles Julius Francis in hunting costume as a mediaeval monseigneur with a hooded falcon on his wrist. I awoke to find directly in my line of vision upon the shelf of the alcove in front of me the solid phalanx of the ten volumes of Larousse's "Grand Dictionaire Universe du XIX Siècle," and I reached forward and pulled down the letter "N." "Nevers"—there it was—"Capitol of the Department of Nievre. Ducal palace built in 1475. Charles III de Gonzagne, petit-fils de Charles II," had sold the duchy of Nevers and his other domains in France to Cardinal Mazarin "par acte du Jul. 11, 1659." So far so good. The cardinal had left the duchy by will to Philippe Jules François Mancini, his nephew, who had died May 8, 1707. Ah! *Julius Francis*! It was like meeting an old friend. Philippe Jules François Mancini. Mazarin had obtained letters confirming him in the possession of the Duchy of Nivernais and Donzois in 1720. Then he had died in 1768, leaving the duchy to Louis Jules Barbon Mancini-Mozarini. This son who was the last Duc of Nivernais, had died in 1798! "He was the last of the name," said Larousse. I rubbed my eyes. It was there fast enough—"last of the name." Something was wrong. Without getting up I rang for a copy of "Burke's Peerage."

"Londonderry, Marquess of, married Oct. 2nd, 1875, Lady Theresa Susey Helen, Lady of Grace of St. John of Jerusalem, eldest daughter of the 19th Earl of Shrewsbury." Dear me! "Dudley, Earl of, married September 14, 1891, Rachael, Lady of Grace of the Order of St. John of Jerusalem, youngest daughter of Charles Henry Gurney." I closed the book and began to think, and the more I thought the more I wondered. There really didn't seem particular need of going further. If the fellow was a fraud, he was a fraud, that was all. But how in Heaven's name could a man make up a story like that! That night I dreamed once more of the ducal palace of Nivernais, only its courtyard resembled that of the Tombs and many couples walked in a straggling line beneath its walls.

A day or two passed and I had heard no more of the Duc Charles Julius when one afternoon a lady called at my office and sent in her name as Mrs. de Nevers. She proved to be an attractive young woman a little over twenty, dressed in black, whose face showed that she had suffered more than a little. She explained that her husband was confined in the Tombs on a charge of perjury. But that was not all—he was worse than a perjurer. He was an impostor—*a bigamist*. He had another wife living somewhere in England—in Manchester, she thought. Oh, it was too terrible. He had told her that he was the Count Charles de Nevers, eldest son of the Duc de Nevers—in France, you know. And she had believed him. He had had letters to everybody in Montreal, her home, and plenty of money and beautiful clothes. He had dazzled her completely. The wedding had been quite an affair and presents had come from the Duke and Duchess of Nevers, from the Marchioness of Londonderry and from the Countess of Dudley. There were also letters from the Prince and Princess of Aremberg (in Belgium) and the Counts André and Fernand of Nevers. It had all been so wonderful and romantic! Then they had gone on their wedding journey and had been ecstatically happy. In Chicago, they had been received with open arms. That was before the death of the Duke—yes, her mourning was for the Duke. She smiled sadly. I think she still more than half believed that she was a duchess—and she deserved to be if ever any girl did. Then all of a sudden their money had given out and the Duke had been arrested for not paying their hotel bill. Perhaps I would like to see a newspaper clipping? It was dreadful! She was ashamed to be seen anywhere after that. She had even been obliged to pawn his cross of the Legion of Honor, the Leopold Cross of Belgium, and another beautiful decoration which he had been accustomed to wear when they went out to dinner. This was the clipping:

CHICAGO SOCIETY THE DUPE OF BOGUS COUNT
HOTEL AND SEVERAL WHILOM FRIENDS FILLED WITH REGRET—THE "COUNT" ARRESTED

Chicago, Jan. 29.—"Count Charles Julius François de Nevers" was in the Police court to-day for defrauding the Auditorium Annex of a board bill. The Count came to the French Consul, M. Henri Meron, amply supplied with credentials. He posed as Consulting Engineer of the United States Steel Corporation. He was introduced into all the clubs, including the Alliance Française, where he was entertained and spoke on literature.

He was accompanied by a charming young "Countess," and the honors showered upon them and the adulation paid by society tuft-hunters was something they will never forget.

They returned the entertainments. The Count borrowed several thousand dollars.

President Furber, of the Olympic Games, said to-day of the "Count:"

"This man confided to me that he had invented a machine for perpetual motion, the chief difficulty of which was that it accumulated energy so fast that it could not be controlled. He asked me to invest in some of his schemes, which I refused to do."

The fate of the Count is still pending and he was led back to a cell. He has been a week behind the bars. The "Countess" is in tears.

"The Countess is me," she explained.

"Was he sent to prison?" I asked.

"Oh, no," she answered. "You see they really couldn't tell whether he was a Count or not, so they had to let him go."

"He ought to be hung!" I cried.

"I really think he ought," she answered. "You see it is quite embarrassing, because legally I have never been married at all, have I?"

"I don't know," I answered, lying like a gentleman. "Time enough to look that up later."

"I found out afterwards," she said, apparently somewhat encouraged, "that his first wife was a nurse maid in London."

"Yes," said I, "he told me so himself."

Just then there came a knock at my door and O'Toole appeared.

"How are you, Counsellor," he said with a grin. "You know Charley Nevers, well, av all the pious frauds! Say, Counsellor, ain't he the cute feller! What do you suppose, now? I got his record to-day. Cast yer eye over it."

I did. This is it:
No. 98
No. B 7721
The Central Office,
Bureau of Detectives,
Police Department of the City of New York,
300 Mulberry Street.
Name......................Charles François
Alias......................Count de Nevers
Date of Arrest.............1903
Place of Arrest............London, England
Cause of Arrest............False Pretenses
Name of Court..............Sessions
To what Prison.............Penal Servitude
Term of Imprisonment........Eighteen months.
REMARKS: Fraudulently obtained motor-car in London under pretense that he was Charles Duke de Nevers, son of Oscar, Prince de Nevers."

"So he's an ex-convict!" I exclaimed.

"He's more than that!" cried O'Toole. "He's a bir-rd!"

I turned to Mrs. de Nevers or whoever she legally was.

"How did he come to do such a foolish thing as to offer to go on the bail bond of a perfect stranger? What good could it do him? He was sure to be caught."

"I don't know," said she. "He was always doing things like that. He wanted to seem fine and grand, I guess. We always travelled in style. Why, the afternoon he signed the bond he came home and told me how the police had been troubling a gentleman who had a lady with him in an automobile and how he was able to settle the whole affair without the slightest difficulty and send them on their way. He was quite pleased about it."

"But why do you suppose be did it?"

"He just thought he'd do 'em a favor," suggested O'Toole, "and in that way get in wid 'em an' take their money later, mebbe!"

"Who is he? Do you know?" I asked the girl.

"I haven't the vaguest idea!" she sighed.

A week later Charles Julius Francis stood at the bar of justice convicted of perjury. His degradation had wrought no change in the dignity of his bearing or the impassiveness of his general appearance, and he received the sentence of the Court without a tremor, and with shoulders thrown back and head erect as befitted a scion of a noble house.

"There's just one thing for me to do with you, Charles Francis," said the Judge rudely, "And that is to send you to State Prison for a term of five years at hard labor."

Francis made no sign.

"There is one other thing I should like to know, however," continued His Honor, "And that is who you really are."

The prisoner bowed slightly.

"I am Charles Julius Francis," he replied quietly, "Duc de Nevers, and Commander of the Legion of Honor."

VIII
A Finder of Missing Heirs

The professional prosecutor is continually surprised at the insignificant amount of crime existing in comparison with the extraordinary scope of criminal opportunity. To be sure, the number of crimes actually detected is infinitesimal as contrasted with those committed, but even so the conviction constantly grows that the world is astonishingly honest when one considers the unlikelihood that any specific prospective offence will be discovered. How few dishonest servants there are, for example, out of the million or so composing that class of persons who have an unlimited opportunity to snap up not only unconsidered trifles, but personal property of great value. The actual honesty of the servants is probably greater than that of the masters—in the final analysis.

Men are not only "presumed to be innocent" in the eyes of the law, but are found to be so, as a matter of daily experience, so far as honesty in the ordinary affairs of life is concerned, and the fact that we rely so implicitly upon the truthfulness and integrity of our fellows is the principal reason why violations of this imperative social law should be severely dealt with. If it were possible adequately to determine or deal with any such issue mere lying should be made a crime.

It is matter of constant wonder that shrewd business men will put through all sorts of deals, when thousands of dollars are at stake, relying entirely upon the word of some single person, whom they do not in fact know. John Smith is looking for a house. He finds one he likes with an old lady, who says her name is Sarah Jones, living in it, and offers her forty thousand dollars for her real estate. She accepts. His lawyer searches the title and finds that Sarah Jones is the owner of record. The old lady is invited to the lawyer's office, executes a warranty deed, and goes off with the forty thousand dollars. Now in a great number of instances no one really knows whether the aged dame is Sarah Jones or not; and she perhaps may be, and sometimes is, only the caretaker's second cousin, who is looking after the house in the latter's absence.

There are thousands of acres of land and hundreds of millions of money waiting at compound interest to be claimed by unknown heirs or next of kin. Even if the real ones cannot be found one would think that this defect could be easily supplied by some properly ingenious person.

"My Uncle Bill went to sea in '45 and was never heard from again. Will you find out if he left any money?" wrote a client to the author. Careful search failed to reveal any money. But if the money had been found *first* how easy it would have been to turn up a nephew! Yet the industry of producing properly authenticated nephews, heirs, legatees, next of kin and claimants of all sorts has never been adequately developed. There are plenty of "agents" who for a moderate fee will inform you whether or not there is a fortune waiting for you, but there is no agency within the writer's knowledge which will supply an heir for every fortune. From a business point of view the idea seems to have possibilities.

Some few years after the Civil War a Swede named Ebbe Petersen emigrated to this country to better his condition. Fortune smiled upon him and he amassed a modest bank account, which, with considerable foresight, he invested in a large tract of unimproved land in the region known as "The Bronx," New York City.

In the summer of 1888 Petersen determined to take a vacation and revisit Sweden, and accordingly deeded all his real estate to his wife. Just before starting he decided to take his wife and only child, a little girl of ten or twelve, with him. Accordingly they set sail from Hoboken Saturday, August 11, upon the steamer *Geiser*, of the Thingvalla Line, bound for Copenhagen. At four o'clock Tuesday morning, at a point thirty miles south of Sable Island and two hundred miles out of Halifax, the *Geiser*, in the midst of a thick fog, crashed suddenly into a sister ship, the *Thingvalla*, of the same line, and sank. The *Thingvalla* was herself badly crippled, but, after picking up thirty-one survivors, managed to limp into Halifax, from which port the rescued were brought to New York. Only fourteen of the *Geiser's* passengers had been saved and the Petersens were not among them. They were never heard of again, and no relatives came forward to claim their property, which, happening to be in the direct line of the city's development, was in course of time mapped out into streets and house lots and became exceedingly valuable. Gradually houses were built upon it, various people bought it for investment, and it took on the look of other semi-developed suburban property.

In the month of December, 1905, over seventeen years after the sinking of the *Geiser*, a lawyer named H. Huffman Browne, offered to sell "at a bargain" to a young architect named Benjamin Levitan two house lots adjacent to the southwest corner of One Hundred and Seventy-fourth Street and Monroe Avenue, New York City. It so happened that Browne had, not long before, induced Levitan to go into another real-estate deal, in which the architect's suspicions had been aroused by finding that the property alleged by the lawyer to be "improved" was, in fact, unbuilt upon. He had lost no money in the original transaction, but he determined that no such mistake should occur a second time, and he accordingly visited the property, and also had a search made of the title, which revealed the fact that Browne was not the record owner, as he had stated, but that, on the contrary, the land stood in the name of "William R. Hubert."

It should be borne in mind that both the parties to this proposed transaction were men well known in their own professions. Browne, particularly, was a real-estate lawyer of some distinction, and an editor of what were known as the old "New York Civil Procedure Reports." He was a middle-aged man, careful in his dress, particular in his speech, modest and quiet in his demeanor, by reputation a gentleman and a scholar, and had practised at the New York bar some twenty-five years.

But Levitan, who had seen many wolves in sheep's clothing, and had something of the Sherlock Holmes in his composition, determined to seek the advice of the District Attorney, and having done so, received instructions to go ahead and consummate the purchase of the property. He, therefore, informed Browne that he had learned that the latter was not the owner of record, to which Browne replied that that was true, but that the property really did belong to him in fact, being recorded in Hubert's name merely as a matter of convenience (because Hubert was unmarried), and that, moreover, he, Browne, had an unrecorded deed from Hubert to himself, which he would produce, or would introduce Hubert to Levitan and let him execute a deed direct. Levitan assented to the latter proposition, and the fourteenth of December, 1905, was fixed as the date for the delivery of the deeds and the payment for the property.

At two o'clock in the afternoon of that day Browne appeared at Levitan's office (where a detective was already in attendance) and stated that he had been unable to procure Mr. Hubert's personal presence, but had received from him deeds, duly executed, to the property. These he offered to Levitan. At this moment the detective stepped forward, took possession of the papers, and invited the lawyer to accompany him to the District Attorney's office. To this Browne offered no opposition, and the party adjourned to the Criminal Courts Building, where Mr. John W. Hart, an Assistant District Attorney, accused him of having obtained money from Levitan by means of false pretenses as to the ownership of the property, and requested from him an explanation. Browne replied without hesitation that he could not understand why this charge should be made against him; that he had, in fact, received the deeds from Mr. Hubert only a short time before he had delivered them to Levitan; that Mr. Hubert was in New York; that he was the owner of the property, and that no fraud of any sort had been attempted or intended.

Mr. Hart now examined the supposed deeds and found that the signatures to them, as well as the signatures to a certain affidavit of title, which set forth that William R. Hubert was a person of substance, had all been executed before a notary, Ella F. Braman, on that very day. He therefore sent at once for Mrs. Braman who, upon her arrival, immediately and without hesitation, positively identified the defendant, H. Huffman Browne, as the person who had executed the papers before her an hour or so before. The case on its face seemed clear enough. Browne had apparently deliberately forged William R. Hubert's name, and it did not even seem necessary that Mr. Hubert should be summoned as a witness, since the property was recorded in his name, and Browne himself had stated that Hubert was then actually in New York.

But Browne indignantly protested his innocence. It was clear, he insisted, that Mrs. Braman was mistaken, for why, in the name of common-sense, should he, a lawyer of standing, desire to forge Hubert's name, particularly when he himself held an unrecorded deed of the same property, and could have executed a good conveyance to Levitan had the latter so desired. Such a performance would have been utterly without an object. But the lawyer was nervous, and his description of Hubert as "a wealthy mine owner from the West, who owned a great deal of property in New York, and had an office in the Flatiron Building," did not ring convincingly in Mr. Hart's ears. The Assistant District Attorney called up the janitor of the building in question on the telephone. But no such person had an office there. Browne, much flustered, said the janitor was either a fool or a liar. He had been at Hubert's office that very morning. He offered to go and find him in twenty minutes. But Mr. Hart thought that the lawyer had better make his explanation before a magistrate, and caused his arrest and commitment on a charge of forgery. Little did he suspect what an ingenious fraud was about to be unearthed.

The days went by and Browne stayed in the Tombs, unable to raise the heavy bail demanded, but no Hubert appeared. Meantime the writer, to whom the case had been sent for trial, ordered a complete search of the title to the property, and in a week or so became possessed, to his amazement, of a most extraordinary and complicated collection of facts.

He discovered that the lot of land offered by Browne to Levitan, and standing in Hubert's name, was originally part of the property owned by Ebbe Petersen, the unfortunate Swede who, with his family, had perished in the *Geiser* off Cape Sable in 1888.

The title search showed that practically all of the Petersen property had been conveyed by Mary A. Petersen to a person named Ignatius F. X. O'Rourke, by a deed, which purported to have been executed on June 27, 1888, about two weeks before the Petersens sailed for Copenhagen, and which was signed with Mrs. Petersen's mark, but that this deed had not been recorded until July 3, 1899, *eleven years* after the loss of the *Geiser*.

The writer busied himself with finding some one who had known Mrs. Petersen, and by an odd coincidence discovered a woman living in the Bronx who had been an intimate friend and playmate of the little Petersen girl. This witness, who was but a child when the incident had occurred, clearly recalled the fact that Ebbe Petersen had not decided to take his wife and daughter with him on the voyage until a few days before they sailed. They had then invited her, the witness—now a Mrs. Cantwell—to go with them, but her mother had declined to allow her to do so. Mrs. Petersen, moreover, according to Mrs. Cantwell, was a woman of education, who wrote a particularly fine hand. Other papers were discovered executed at about the same time, signed by Mrs. Petersen with her full name. It seemed inconceivable that she should have signed any deed, much less one of so much importance, with her *mark*, and, moreover, that she should have executed any such deed at all when her husband was on the spot to convey his own property.

But the strangest fact of all was that the attesting witness to this extraordinary instrument was H. Huffman Browne! It also appeared to have been recorded *at his instance* eleven years after its execution.

In the meantime, however, that is to say, between the sinking of the *Geiser* in '88 and the recording of Mary Petersen's supposed deed in '99, another *equally mysterious* deed to the same property had been filed. This document, executed and recorded in 1896, purported to convey part of the Petersen property to a man named John J. Keilly, and was signed by a person calling himself Charles A. Clark. By a later deed, executed and signed a few days later, John J. Keilly appeared to have conveyed the same property to Ignatius F. X. O'Rourke, the very person to whom Mrs. Petersen had apparently executed her deed in 1888. And H. Huffman Browne was the attesting witness to both these deeds!

A glance at the following diagram will serve to clear up any confusion which may exist in the mind of the reader:

```
      1888  MARY A. PETERSEN   1896  CHARLES A. CLARK
(Not       by her (X) deed          conveys same property
Recorded   conveys to               to
until 1899) I.F.X. O'ROURKE          JOHN J. KEILLY.
     |
     |                1896  JOHN J. KEILLY
     |                      conveys to
     |                      I.F.X. O'ROURKE
     |_____|
```

O'ROURKE thus holds land through two sources.

Browne was the witness to both these parallel transactions! Of course it was simple enough to see what had occurred. In 1896 a mysterious man, named Clark, without vestige of right or title, so far as the records showed, had conveyed Ebbe Petersen's property to a man named Keilly, equally unsubstantial, who had passed it over to one O'Rourke. Then Browne had suddenly recorded Mrs. Petersen's deed giving O'Rourke the very same property. Thus this O'Rourke, whoever he may have been, held all the Petersen property by two chains of title, one through Clark and Keilly, and the other through Mrs. Petersen. Then he had gone ahead and deeded it all away to various persons, through one of whom William R. Hubert had secured his title. But every deed on record which purported to pass any fraction of the Petersen property was witnessed by H. Huffman Browne! And Browne was the attesting witness to the deed under which Hubert purported to hold. Thus the chain of title, at the end of which Levitan found himself, ran back to Mary Petersen, with H. Huffman Browne peering behind the arras of every signature.

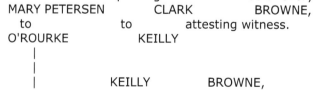

```
MARY PETERSEN        CLARK           BROWNE,
    to             to          attesting witness.
 O'ROURKE          KEILLY
    |
    |
    |          KEILLY           BROWNE,
```

```
|          to          attesting witness.
|       O'ROURKE
|          |
|_____|
```

O'ROURKE
to
WILLIAM P. COLLITON

BROWNE,
attesting witness.

WILLIAM P. COLLITON
to
JOHN GARRETSON

BROWNE,
attesting witness.

JOHN GARRETSON
to
HERMAN BOLTE

BROWNE,
attesting witness.

HERMAN BOLTE
to
BENJ. FREEMAN

BROWNE,
attesting witness.

BENJ. FREEMAN
to
WILLIAM R. HUBERT

BROWNE,
attesting witness.

The Assistant District Attorney rubbed his forehead and wondered who in thunder all these people were. Who, for example, to begin at the beginning, was Charles A. Clark, and why should he be deeding away Ebbe Petersen's property? And who were Keilly and O'Rourke, and all the rest—Colliton, Garretson, Bolte and Freeman? And who, for that matter, was Hubert?

A score of detectives were sent out to hunt up these elusive persons, but, although the directories of twenty years were searched, no Charles A. Clark, John J. Keilly or I. F. X. O'Rourke could be discovered. Nor could any one named Colliton, Freeman or Hubert be found. The only persons who did appear to exist were Garretson and Bolte.

Quite by chance the Assistant District Attorney located the former of these, who proved to be one of Browne's clients, and who stated that he had taken title to the property at the lawyer's request and as a favor to him, did not remember from whom he had received it, had paid nothing for it, received nothing for it, and had finally deeded it to Herman Bolte at the direction of Browne. Herman Bolte, an ex-judge of the Municipal Court, who had been removed for misconduct in office, admitted grumblingly that, while at, one time he had considered purchasing the property in question, he had never actually done so, that the deed from Garretson to himself had been recorded without his knowledge or his authority, that he had paid nothing for the property and had received nothing for it, and had, at the instruction of Browne, conveyed it to

Benjamin Freeman. Garretson apparently had never seen Bolte, and Bolte had never seen Freeman, while William R. Hubert, the person to whom the record showed Freeman had transferred the property, remained an invisible figure, impossible to reduce to tangibility.

Just what Browne had attempted to do—had done—was obvious. In some way, being a real-estate lawyer, he had stumbled upon the fact that this valuable tract of land lay unclaimed. Accordingly, he had set about the easiest way to reduce it to possession. To make assurance doubly sure he had forged two chains of title, one through an assumed heir and the other through the owner herself. Then he had juggled the title through a dozen or so grantees, and stood ready to dispose of the property to the highest bidder.

There he stayed in the Tombs, demanding a trial and protesting his innocence, and asserting that if the District Attorney would only look long enough he would find William R. Hubert. But an interesting question of law had cropped up to delay matters.

Of course, if there was anybody by the name of Hubert who actually owned the property, and Browne had signed his name, conveying the same, to a deed to Levitan, Browne was guilty of forgery in the first degree. But the evidence in the case pointed toward the conclusion that Browne himself *was* Hubert. If this was so, how could Browne be said to have forged the name of Hubert, when he had a perfect legal right to take the property under any name he chose to assume? This was incontestable. If your name be Richard Roe you may purchase land and receive title thereto under the name of John Doe, and convey it under that name without violating the law. This as a general proposition is true so long as the taking of a fictitious name is for an honest purpose and not tainted with fraud. The Assistant District Attorney felt that the very strength of his case created, as it were, a sort of "legal weakness," for the more evidence he should put in against Browne, the clearer it would become that Hubert was merely Browne himself, and this would necessitate additional proof that Browne had taken the property in the name of Hubert for purposes of fraud, which could only be established by going into the whole history of the property. Of course, if Browne were so foolish as to put in the defence that Hubert really existed, the case would be plain sailing. If, however, Browne was as astute as the District Attorney believed him to be, he might boldly admit that there was no Hubert except himself, and that in taking title to the property and disposing thereof under that name, he was committing no violation of law for which he could be prosecuted.

The case was moved for trial on the twelfth of March, 1906, before Judge Warren W. Foster, in Part Three of the Court of General Sessions in New York. The defendant was arraigned at the bar without counsel, owing to the absence of his lawyer through sickness, and Mr. Lewis Stuyvesant Chanler, the later Lieutenant-Governor of the State, was assigned to defend him. At this juncture Browne arose and addressed the Court. In the most deferential and conciliatory manner he urged that he was entitled to an adjournment until such time as he could produce

William R. Hubert as a witness; stating that, although the latter had been in town on December 14th, and had personally given him the deeds in question, which he had handed to Levitan, Hubert's interests in the West had immediately called him from the city, and that he was then in Goldfields, Nevada; that since he had been in the Tombs he, Browne, had been in correspondence with a gentleman by the name of Alfred Skeels, of the Teller House, Central City, Colorado, from whom he had received a letter within the week to the effect that Hubert had arranged to start immediately for New York, for the purpose of testifying as a witness for the defence. The prosecutor thereupon demanded the production of this letter from the alleged Skeels, and Browne was compelled to state that he had immediately destroyed it on its receipt. The prosecutor then argued that under those circumstances, and in view of the fact that the People's evidence showed conclusively that no such person as Hubert existed, there was no reason why the trial should not proceed then and there. The Court thereupon ruled that the case should go on.

A jury was procured after some difficulty, and the evidence of Mr. Levitan received, showing that Browne had represented Hubert to be a man of substance, and had produced an affidavit, purported to be sworn to by Hubert, to the same effect, with deeds alleged to have been signed by him. Mrs. Braman then swore that upon the same day Browne had himself acknowledged these very deeds and had sworn to the affidavit before her as a notary, under the name of William R. Hubert.

Taken with the fact that Browne had in open court stated that Hubert was a living man, this made out a *prima facie* case. But, of course, the District Attorney was unable to determine whether or not Browne would take the stand in his own behalf, or what his defence would be, and, in order to make assurance doubly sure, offered in evidence all the deeds to the property in question, thereby establishing the fact that it was originally part of the Petersen estate, and disclosing the means whereby it had eventually been recorded in the name of Hubert.

The prosecution then rested its case, and the burden shifted to the defence to explain how all these deeds, attested by Browne, came to be executed and recorded. It was indeed a difficult, if not impossible, task which the accused lawyer undertook when he went upon the stand. He again positively and vehemently denied that he had signed the name of Hubert to the deed which he had offered to Levitan, and persisted in the contention that Hubert was a real man, who sooner or later would turn up. He admitted knowing the Petersen family in a casual way, and said he had done some business for them, but stated that he had not heard of their tragic death until some years after the sinking of the *Geiser*. He had then ascertained that no one had appeared to lay claim to Mrs. Petersen's estate, and he had accordingly taken it upon himself to adveritse for heirs. In due course Charles A. Clark had appeared and had deeded the property to Keilly, who in turn had conveyed it to O'Rourke. Just who this mysterious O'Rourke was he could not explain, nor could he account in any satisfactory manner for the recording in 1899 of the deed signed with Mary Petersen's mark. He said that it had "turned up" in O'Rourke's hands after O'Rourke had become possessed of the property through the action of the heirs, and that he had no recollection of ever having seen it before or having witnessed it. In the latter transactions, by which the property had been split up, he claimed to have acted only as attorney for the different grantors. He was unable to give the address or business of O'Rourke, Clark, Keilly or Freeman, and admitted that he had never seen any of them save at his own office. He was equally vague as to Hubert, whose New York residence he gave as 111 Fifth Avenue. No such person, however, had ever been known at that address.

With the exception of the upper left hand signature and the four immediately below it of H. Huffman Browne, these are all the signatures of imaginary persons invented by Browne to further his schemes. The upper right-hand slip shows the signatures to the Wilson bond, among which appears that of W.R. Hubert.

Browne gave his testimony in the same dry, polite and careful manner in which he had always been accustomed to discuss his cases and deliver his arguments. It seemed wholly impossible to believe that this respectable-looking person could be a dangerous character, yet the nature of his offence and the consequences of it were apparent when the State called to the stand an old broom-maker, who had bought from Browne one of the lots belonging to the Petersen estate. Holding up three stumps where fingers should have been, he cried out, choking with tears:

"My vriends, for vifteen years I vorked at making brooms—me und my vife—from fife in the morning until six at night, und I loose mine fingern trying to save enough money to puy a house that we could call our own. Then when we saved eight hundred dollars this man come to us und sold us a lot. We were very happy. Yesterday anoder man served me mit a paper that we must leave our house, because we did not own the land! We must go away! Where? We haf no place to go. Our home is being taken from us, und that man [pointing his stumps at Browne]—that man has stolen it from us!"

He stopped, unable to speak. The defendant's lawyer properly objected, but, with this piece of testimony ringing in their ears, it is hardly surprising that the jury took but five minutes to convict Browne of forgery in the first degree.

A few days later the judge sentenced him to twenty years in State's prison.

Then other people began to wake up. The Attorney-General guessed that the Petersen property had all escheated to the State, the Swedish Government sent a deputy to make inquiries, the Norwegian Government was sure that he was a Norwegian, and the Danish that he was a Dane. No one knows yet who is the real owner, and there are half a dozen heirs squatting on every corner of it. Things are much worse than before Browne tried to sell the ill-fated lot to Levitan, but a great many people who were careless before are careful now.

It soon developed, however, that lawyer Browne's industry and ingenuity had not been confined to the exploitation of the estate of Ebbe Petersen. Before the trial was well under way the City Chamberlain of New York notified the District Attorney that a peculiar incident had occurred at his office, in which not only the defendant figured, but William R. Hubert, his familiar, as well. In the year 1904 a judgment had been entered in the Supreme Court, which adjudged that a certain George Wilson was entitled to a one-sixth interest in the estate of Jane Elizabeth Barker, recently deceased. George Wilson had last been heard of, twenty years before, as a farmhand, in Illinois, and his whereabouts were at this time unknown. Suddenly, however, he had appeared. That is to say, H. Huffman Browne had appeared as his attorney, and demanded his share of the property which had been deposited to his credit with the City Chamberlain and amounted to seventy-five hundred dollars. The lawyer had presented a petition signed apparently by Wilson and a bond also subscribed by him, to which had been appended the names of certain sureties. One of these was a William R. Hubert—the same William R. Hubert who had mysteriously disappeared when his presence was so vital to the happiness and liberty of his creator. But the City Chamberlain had not been on his guard, and had paid over the seventy-five hundred dollars to Browne without ever having seen the claimant or suspecting for an instant that all was not right.

It was further discovered at the same time that Browne had made several other attempts to secure legacies remaining uncalled for in the city's treasury. In how many cases he had been successful will probably never be known, but it is unlikely that his criminal career dated only from the filing of the forged Petersen deed in 1896.

Browne made an heroic and picturesque fight to secure a reversal of his conviction through all the State courts, and his briefs and arguments are monuments to his ingenuity and knowledge of the law. He alleged that his conviction was entirely due to a misguided enthusiasm on the part of the prosecutor, the present writer, whom he characterized as a "novelist" and dreamer. The whole case, he alleged, was constructed out of the latter's fanciful imagination, a cobweb of suspicion, accusation and falsehood. Some day his friend Hubert would come out of the West, into which he had so unfortunately disappeared, and release an innocent man, sentenced, practically to death, because the case had fallen into the hands of one whose sense of the dramatic was greater than his logic.

Perchance he will. Mayhap, when H. Huffman Browne is the oldest inmate of Sing Sing, or even sooner, some gray-haired figure will appear at the State Capitol, and knock tremblingly at the door of the Executive, asking for a pardon or a rehearing of the case, and claiming to be the only original, genuine William R. Hubert—such a dénouement would not be beyond the realms of possibility, but more likely the request will come in the form of a petition, duly attested and authenticated before some notary in the West, protesting against Browne's conviction and incarceration, and bearing the flowing signature of William R. Hubert— the same signature that appears on Browne's deeds to Levitan—the same that is affixed to the bond of George Wilson, the vanished farmhand, claimant to the estate of Jane Elizabeth Barker.

IX.
A Murder Conspiracy[4]

William M. Rice, eighty-four years of age, died at the Berkshire Apartments at 500 Madison Avenue, New York City, at about half after seven o'clock on the evening of Sunday, September 23, 1900. He had been ill for some time, but it was expected that he would recover. On or about the moment of his death, two elderly ladies, friends of the old gentleman, had called at the house with cakes and wine, to see him. The elevator man rang the bell of Mr. Rice's apartment again and again, but could elicit no response, and the ladies, much disappointed, went away. While the bell was ringing Charles F. Jones, the confidential valet of the aged man, was waiting, he says, in an adjoining room until a cone saturated with chloroform, which he had placed over the face of his sleeping master, should effect his death.

Did Jones murder Rice? If so, was it, as he claims, at the instigation of Albert T. Patrick?

These two questions, now settled in the affirmative forever, so far as criminal and civil litigation are concerned, have been the subject of private study and public argument for more than seven years.

Mr. Rice was a childless widower, living the life of a recluse, attended only by Jones, who was at once his secretary, valet and general servant. No other person lived in the apartment, and few visitors ever called there. Patrick was a New York lawyer with little practice who had never met Mr. Rice, was employed as counsel in litigation hostile to him, yet in whose favor a will purporting to be signed by Rice, June 30, 1900, turned up after the latter's death, by the terms of which Patrick came into the property, amounting to over seven million dollars, in place of a charitable institution named in an earlier will of 1896. It is now universally admitted that the alleged will of 1900 was a forgery, as well as four checks drawn to Patrick's order (two for $25,000 each, one for $65,000, and one for $135,000, which represented practically all of Rice's bank accounts), an order giving him control of the contents of Rice's safe deposit vaults (in which were more than $2,500,000 in securities), and also a general assignment by which he became the owner of Rice's entire estate. Thus upon Rice's death Patrick had every possible variety of document necessary to possess himself of the property. Jones took nothing under any of these fraudulent instruments. Hence Patrick's motive in desiring the death of Rice is the foundation stone of the case against him. But that Patrick desired and would profit by Rice's death in no way tends to establish that Rice did not die a natural death. Patrick would profit equally whether Rice died by foul means or natural, and the question as to whether murder was done must be determined from other evidence. This is only to be found in the confession of the valet Jones and in the testimony of the medical experts who performed the autopsy. Jones, a self-confessed murderer, swears that upon the advice and under the direction of Patrick (though in the latter's absence) he killed his master by administering chloroform. There is no direct corroborative evidence save that of the experts. Upon Jones's testimony depended the question of Patrick's conviction or acquittal, and of itself this was not sufficient, for being that of an accomplice it must, under the New York law, be corroborated.

In the confession of Jones the State had sufficient *direct* evidence of the crime and of Patrick's connection with it, providing there was *other evidence tending to connect Patrick with its commission*. This corroborative evidence is largely supplied by the facts which show that for a long time Patrick conspired with Jones to steal the bulk of Mr. Rice's estate at his death. This evidence not only shows Patrick's possible motive for planning Mr. Rice's *murder*, but also tends to corroborate Jones's whole story of the conspiracy.

Rice did not know Patrick even by sight. He had heard of him only as a person retained by another lawyer (Holt) to do "the dirty work" in an action brought by Rice against Holt, as executor, to set aside Mrs. Rice's will, in which she assumed, under the "Community Law" of Texas, where Rice had formerly resided, to dispose of some $2,500,000 of Rice's property. If Rice was a *resident of Texas* she had the legal right to do this,—otherwise not. Holt employed Patrick to get evidence that Rice still was such a resident. Rice knew of this and hated Patrick.

Patrick's connection with the Rice litigation had begun four years before the murder, which was not planned until August, 1900, His first visit to Rice's apartment was made under the assumed name of Smith for the purpose of discovering whether the valet could be corrupted into furnishing fictitious proof of Rice's intent to reside in Texas. He flattered Jones; told him he was underpaid and not appreciated, and, after a second visit, at which he disclosed his right name, persuaded him to typewrite a letter on Rice's stationery addressed to Baker, Botts, Baker & Lovett (Rice's attorneys), in which he should be made to say that he had lost hope of winning the suit against Holt, was really a citizen of Texas, and wanted to settle the litigation. Patrick said that he could arrange for the signing of such a letter and was willing to pay Jones $250 for his help. Jones agreed.

Patrick now learned that Mr. Rice was living with no companion except Jones; that he held little communication with the outside world; that the valet was in his confidence and thoroughly familiar with his papers, and that the will made in 1896 disinherited natural heirs in favor of an educational institution which he had founded in Texas. He also learned that while Mr. Rice was 84 years of age he was in possession of all his faculties, conducted his own business, and might live for years. Possessed of these facts Patrick's evil mind soon developed a conspiracy with Jones to secure the whole estate.

Mr. Rice's pet charity was the William M. Rice Institute "for the advance of science, art and literature," of Texas, which he had founded in 1891. He had donated to it more than a million and a half dollars. By the will of 1896 only small legacies were bequeathed to relatives, while the bulk of his fortune was left to the Institute.

About a month after Patrick's first visit to the Berkshire Apartments, that is, in December, 1899, while he and Jones were examining Rice's private papers, they stumbled upon the will. Patrick saw his opportunity. By the forgery of a new will which would increase the legacies of those mentioned in the will of 1896 and leave legacies to every person who might have any claim upon the estate, it would be for the interest of those persons to sustain and carry into effect the forgery. The whole scheme was based upon the belief that "every man has his price." He told Jones that he thought the will unjust; that he did not think it right to leave so little to relatives, and later he brought to Jones a rough draft of a will which could be substituted for the genuine one. Patrick was to get half the estate, the relatives were to receive double or three times the amount provided in the 1896 will, and what was left was to be given to the Rice Institute. He proposed that Jones should typewrite this will, and guaranteed to arrange for the witnessing and signing of it, and promised that Jones should get whatever he wanted. Jones at first objected, but was finally won over. Rewritten many times to include new ideas of the conspirators, the document finally reached the form of the will of June 30, 1900, in which Patrick substituted himself for the Rice Institute and made himself one of the executors.

An ingenious part of the conspiracy was the decision to leave the 1896 will in existence. If Patrick had destroyed it and the relatives had succeeded in overthrowing the will of 1900, the estate would have been left without testamentary disposition and the relatives would have got more than was provided by either will. With the will of 1896 in existence, however, the relatives would get less if they overthrew the forgery. By retaining it, therefore, Patrick figured that the relatives would have selfish reasons for accepting the forgery as genuine.

The preparation of this bogus will occupied about a month, and the next question was the procurement of witnesses. It was desirable to get the same persons who witnessed the former will. These were Walter H. Wetherbee and W. F. Harmon, clerks for many years at Swenson's banking house. On the assumption that Wetherbee had been injured by Rice and was therefore hostile to him, Jones practically unfolded the scheme. He told Wetherbee that one of Mr. Rice's bonds had disappeared and that Rice had accused Wetherbee of stealing it. He wound up with the suggestion, "I will get one witness and you can get another, and the thing is done." But Wetherbee indignantly declined to join in the conspiracy.

Morris Meyers, who had been employed in Patrick's office, and David L. Short, a friend of both, were the false witnesses finally selected.

They were clothed with the appearance of honesty and were brought into contact with Rice by Jones at various times: Meyers as a notary public, and Short as commissioner of deeds for the State of Texas, an appointment procured for him by Patrick probably for this specific purpose.

The date of the forged will, June 30, 1900, was selected to correspond with the date of three genuine papers which Rice acknowledged before Short on that date.

Last page of the forged will of 1900, showing the forgery of Rice's signature, and the false attestation of Short and Meyers.

The next step was to obviate the absurdity of Patrick's being selected as the residuary legatee at a time when he was engaged in bitter litigation against Rice. The best way out was for Patrick to pose as a lawyer who had brought about a settlement of this expensive litigation and thus won Rice's regard. Patrick first tried to accomplish this by getting friends to visit Rice and urge a settlement. But Rice rebuffed them all. Accordingly, Patrick again resorted to forgery, and in August, 1900, manufactured an instrument of settlement, dated March 6, 1900.

But such an agreement would not explain the paradox of a man whom Rice hated and despised and did not know by sight turning up as the principal beneficiary under his will. It was necessary to manufacture evidence to be used after Rice's death in support of his claim of close relations. The idea of a personal meeting with Rice had been abandoned on Jones's advice, and Patrick therefore caused the valet to prepare twenty-five or thirty forged letters addressed to him and purporting to come from Rice. These referred to current business matters and conveyed the impression that it was Rice's custom to seek the lawyer's advice. One instructed Patrick as to the terms of the will of 1900. Carbon copies were made for filing in Rice's letter book after his death.

To make assurance doubly sure and to secure immediate possession of Rice's securities a general assignment to Patrick of all Rice's estate was forged, and an order giving him access to and possession of the securities on deposit in Rice's safety vault.

But Patrick did not stop here. He procured from Jones three checks signed by Mr. Rice in the regular course of business, one payable to Jones for his July salary and the other two for the July and August salary of an employee of Rice's in Texas named Cohn. These three checks Patrick kept as models, forwarding to Cohn two forged checks filled out by Jones upon which Rice's signature had been traced, and returning to Jones a substitute check with Rice's signature traced upon it. All three checks passed through the banks unsuspected. Traced signatures were also substituted for genuine ones upon letters dictated by Rice to his Texas correspondents. Thus Patrick secured the circulation of five copies of Rice's signature which, if occasion demanded, he could produce as standards of comparison to correspond with his other forgeries. The principal preparations were complete. But title under the will might long be delayed and perhaps even eventually fail. Patrick was poor and in no condition to conduct adequately a serious litigation. The moment Mr. Rice died a large amount of cash would be necessary. For the procurement of this Patrick and Jones looked to the current balance of Rice's bank account, which amounted to some two hundred and fifty thousand dollars on deposit at Swenson's private bank and at the Fifth Avenue Trust Company. With this they felt reasonably secure of success. For even if the will should be set aside as fraudulent they had a second line of defense in the general assignment of the estate and the orders to Rice's two million five hundred thousand dollars of securities.

While the evidence affords a motive for Patrick to desire the death of Mr. Rice, it does not of itself, up to this point, indicate the slightest intention on the part of Patrick to do away with the old gentleman. It was therefore conceded by the prosecution that, upon Jones's own testimony, the conspiracy to murder was not formed until about seven weeks before the event. The first evidence which points to an intent to murder is the famous "cremation letter," dated August 3d.

The cremation letter from Mr. Rice, authorizing Patrick to cremate his body, shows that Patrick intended to do away with Rice in such a way that an autopsy must, if possible, be prevented and the evidence of murder destroyed. That Patrick forged such a letter was evidence that his connection with the murder was premeditated and deliberate. To cremate the body before an autopsy it was necessary to procure a physician's certificate that Rice had died from natural causes. He therefore made preparation to secure such a certificate, and then upon the strength of the cremation letter to give directions for the immediate destruction of the body.

Patrick, with the view of having at hand a physician who would be unsuspicious, and who would issue a certificate of death from natural causes, induced Jones to send for Dr. Curry, his own friend and physician, on an occasion when the valet was ill. This was in March, 1900. Dr. Curry came, and Jones, acting under Patrick's advice, cautioned him not to mention the lawyer's name to Rice. In course of time he saw Rice, gained his good opinion and became his attending physician. But Rice did not die, and curiously enough it was he himself who suggested to Jones the instrumentality of death which was finally employed, for he read an article dealing with the dangers of chloroform as an anaesthetic, and discussed it with the valet. This suggestion was conveyed to Patrick, who asked Dr. Curry whether chloroform left any traces discoverable upon an autopsy. Dr. Curry rather carelessly replied that it left but slight traces if administered only in the quantities which would be fatal to a man with a weak heart. Patrick told Jones, so Jones alleges, to procure some chloroform and this he did, sending to Texas for two bottles of two ounces each. From Dr. Curry's remarks it was manifest that a weakened condition of the patient was an important element, and as Jones was taking some mercury pills (prescribed for him by Dr. Curry), the valet induced his master to take some of them. The old gentleman was benefited, however, rather than weakened. This was *before* the forgery of the cremation letter. It was clear that larger doses of mercury would be necessary, and accordingly Patrick furnished Jones with pellets containing the drug in such quantities that Jones, experimenting with one of them, became ill.

They had now the means to effect gradual death, but as mercury leaves traces discernible at an autopsy, it was decided that the body must be cremated promptly. Hence the cremation letter. It was hoped that Rice might drop off at any moment, owing to his weakened condition, and in anticipation of death Patrick discontinued his visits to the apartment in order to establish a satisfactory alibi. Jones also frequently absented himself from the apartment in the evenings after the old man had fallen asleep.

Last page of the forged will of 1900, showing the forgery of Rice's signature, and the false attestation of Short and Meyers.

On September 16th Rice had an attack of acute indigestion, which might have resulted seriously had it not been for the mercurial pills which promptly relieved him. The reader should observe that practically all of this testimony comes from Jones. There is no extraneous evidence that Patrick induced the giving of the mercury. Patrick, however, spread false rumors as to Rice's general health and also as to his financial condition and intentions, namely, that Rice was only worth seven hundred and fifty thousand dollars, and that those who expected he was going to leave his money to the Institute were doomed to disappointment. But neither his statements about Rice's condition nor his remarks as to the disposition and extent of his property are inconsistent with a mere *hope* that he would die and thus leave Patrick free to enjoy the fruits of his forgeries.

There now occurred, however, an event which may well have played a part in inducing Patrick to supplement forgery by murder. On Sunday, September 16th, the plant of the Merchants' and Planters' Oil Company of Houston, Texas, of which Rice owned seventy-five per cent. of the capital stock, was destroyed by fire. The company being without funds to rebuild, its directors telegraphed to Rice requesting him to advance the money. The amount needed was two hundred and fifty thousand dollars—and if Rice consented, all the available funds on deposit in the New York banks, upon which the conspirators relied to accomplish their object, would be exhausted. Jones endeavored to dissuade the old man from advancing the money, but without effect, and Rice sent a letter to Houston agreeing to supply one hundred and fifty thousand dollars and more in instalments of twenty-five thousand dollars each. This was on September 18th, after he had wired to the same effect on September 17th. Patrick and Jones suppressed a telegram that Rice would advance two hundred and fifty thousand dollars, and on September 19th the old man received word that the first draft in conformity with his telegram of September 17th had been drawn and would arrive in New York on the 22d. Jones says that on showing this to Patrick the latter announced that Rice must be put out of the way as soon as possible. Accordingly, on September 20th and 21st, Jones administered larger doses of mercury than usual, which, while weakening and depressing him, failed to cause his end. Saturday, September 22d, the draft was presented at Rice's apartment. The old man was not confined to his bed, but Jones told the bank messenger, after pretending to consult him, that Rice was too ill to attend to business that day and to return on Monday. That night Jones and Patrick met, and it was agreed (according to Jones) that Rice must not be allowed to survive until Monday. They still hoped that he might die without any further act upon their part, but Jones was informed by Dr. Curry that, although the old man seemed weak and under a great mental strain, he nevertheless thought that he would recover. This Curry also told to Patrick, the latter calling at the doctor's house about five o'clock in the afternoon.

"You think Mr. Rice will be able to go down Monday morning?" Patrick asked.

"You had better wait until Monday morning comes," replied Dr. Curry.

"Do you think he will be able to go down town next week?" persisted the lawyer.

The doctor answered in the affirmative.

That night Mr. Rice slept quietly until eight o'clock Sunday morning. Dr. Curry called and found him in excellent condition, having eaten a hearty breakfast. His heart was a trifle weak, but it was sound. His organs were all working normally; he felt no pain. The doctor left without prescribing any medicine, stating that he would not return unless called, and expressing his opinion that the patient would recover. This was about eleven o'clock, and Jones immediately hastened to Patrick's house and reported the conversation.

It was clear that Rice's death would not occur before Monday morning. He might live to pay over the two hundred and fifty thousand dollars; long enough to give further testimony in the Holt litigation, and thus expose the whole fraudulent scheme of pretended settlement and of friendly relations with the lawyer, and finally, perhaps, even to make a new will. The success of the conspiracy demanded that Rice should die that night. Did he die naturally? Was his death caused by any further act of the conspirators? Did Jones kill him by means of chloroform?

Jones's story is that Patrick supplied him with some oxalic acid which was to be mixed with powdered ammonia and diluted in water, on the theory that it was preferable to chloroform since it would not require Jones's presence in the room at the moment of death. Jones said that he endeavored to administer the mixture to the old man, but that he refused to take it. Jones had already procured the chloroform from Texas, as has been stated, and had turned it over to Patrick. He says that that afternoon he procured this from Patrick, who told him how to administer it. This was a few moments after six o'clock. Rice was sleeping soundly. The colored woman who did the housework was absent for the day and the rooms were deserted. He saturated a sponge with chloroform, constructed a cone out of a towel, placed the sponge in the cone, put the cone over the sleeping man's face and ran out of the room and waited thirty minutes for the chloroform to complete the work. Waiting in the next room he heard the door bell ring, and ring again, but he paid no attention to the summons. In point of fact he was never quite sure himself whether the bell was not the creation of his own overwrought brain. At the end of half an hour he returned to the bedroom, removed the cone from Rice's face and saw that he was dead, then after burning the sponge and the towel in the kitchen range he opened the windows, straightened the rooms out, called the elevator man, asked him to send for Dr. Curry, and telephoned to Patrick that Rice was dead.

Jones had no sooner telephoned Patrick that Rice was dead than the lawyer hastened to Dr. Curry's, and within forty minutes appeared with him in Rice's apartments, assuming complete charge. Summoning an undertaker and having the cremation letter at hand, he gave orders for speedy cremation. But he now discovered the principal mistake in his calculations. He had omitted to investigate the length of time required to heat the crematory. This he now discovered to his horror to be twenty-four hours. But the body must be destroyed. The undertaker suggested that the body might be embalmed while the crematory was being heated, and Patrick at once seized upon the suggestion and gave orders to that effect, although the cremation letter sets forth specifically that one of the reasons why Rice desired cremation was his horror of being embalmed. The body was embalmed at the apartments that night, Dr. Curry innocently supplying the certificate of death from "old age and weak heart," and "as immediate cause, indigestion followed by collocratal diarrhoea with mental worry."

Having arranged for the cremation at the earliest possible moment, Jones and Patrick rifled the trunk in which Rice kept his papers, and stuffed them in a satchel which Patrick bore away with him.

The funeral was to be held early Tuesday morning and the ashes conveyed by Jones to Milwaukee, to be interred near the body of Rice's wife, while the relatives should not be notified until it should be too late for them to reach New York.

The next step was to secure the two hundred and fifty thousand dollars which Rice had on deposit. Patrick had already forged Rice's name to blank checks on Swenson and the Fifth Avenue Trust Company. Early Monday morning Jones, with Patrick looking over his shoulder and directing him, filled out the body of the checks, which covered all but ten thousand dollars of Rice's deposits. These consisted of one for twenty-five thousand dollars and one for sixty-five thousand dollars on Swenson, one for twenty-five thousand dollars and another for one hundred and thirty-five thousand dollars on the Trust Company. They were all made payable to the order of Patrick and dated September 22d, the day before Rice's death. One of the drafts on the Fifth Avenue Trust Company was cashed for him by a friend named Potts early Monday morning, and was paid without suspicion.

But now came the second error, which resulted in the exposure of the conspiracy and conviction for murder. Jones, in filling out the twenty-five thousand dollar check on Swenson, had in his nervousness omitted the "l" from Patrick's Christian name, so that the check read "Abert T. Patrick," and Patrick in his excitement had failed to notice the omission or attempt to obviate it by extra indorsement. This twenty-five thousand dollar Swenson check was intrusted to David L. Short for presentation to Swenson & Sons for certification. When he presented it, Wallace, the clerk, recognized Jones's handwriting in the body of it, and thought the signature looked unnatural. He took it to a rear office, where he showed it to Wetherbee, who was the person whom Jones had approached nine months before with a request that he join the conspiracy to manufacture a bogus will. Wetherbee compared the signature on the check with genuine signatures in the bank, and returned it to Short without any intimation that he regarded it as irregular, but assigning as the reason the defect in the indorsement. Short thereupon returned the check to Patrick, who supplied the necessary supplementary indorsement and telephoned to Jones what had occurred, instructing him to say that the check was all right in case the Swensons should inquire.

Half an hour later Short returned to Swenson's, where the check was examined by one of the firm. Rice's apartments were then called up, and Jones said that the checks were all right. But this did not satisfy Mr. Swenson, so he instructed Wallace to call up the apartment again and insist on talking to Mr. Rice. Jones delayed replying to Wallace and in the afternoon called up Patrick on the telephone, inquiring what he should say. Patrick replied that he would have to say that Rice was dead. And in accordance with this Jones informed Swenson that Rice had died at eight o'clock the previous evening. It was thus clear to Swenson that although the maker of the check was dead, Patrick, a lawyer, cognizant of that fact, was seeking to secure payment upon it. For Jones had told Swenson that he had reported Rice's death to the doctor and to Rice's lawyer, Patrick.

Patrick, accompanied by Potts, went immediately to the bank, where Swenson informed him that the check could be paid only to the administrator. Patrick replied that there would be no administrator; that Rice had left no property in this State, and informed Swenson that he had an assignment by Rice to himself of all Rice's securities with Swenson. He also invited Swenson to the funeral.

Later in the day Patrick attempted to obtain possession of Rice's securities in the Safety Deposit Company and in the Fifth Avenue Trust Company, by presenting forged instruments of transfer and the orders heretofore referred to; but after some delay the trust companies declined him access. The conspiracy had begun to go to pieces. The two mistakes and the failure to secure funds placed Patrick in a dangerous position.

Two o'clock on Monday afternoon, eighteen hours after the death, Jones, at Patrick's direction, began to notify the relatives that Rice had died the evening before, and that the funeral would take place the following morning. The telegrams to Baker and to Rice, Jr., in Texas, were in the following extraordinary form:

Mr. Rice died eight o'clock last night under care of physicians. Death certificate, "old age, weak heart, delirium." Left instructions to be interred in Milwaukee with wife. Funeral 10 A. M. to-morrow at 500 Madison Avenue.

It is significant that care was used to convey the information that the death was a natural one with a physician in attendance; that the body was to be interred in Milwaukee, without reference to the cremation. This may well have been so that if any suspicions of foul play should arise, the recipients, realizing that they could not reach New York in time to arrest matters there, might hasten to Milwaukee to intercept the body, where they could be met by Jones with the cremation letter in his pocket and his urn of ashes under his arm.

But the telegram did arouse suspicion, and Baker and Rice immediately wired Jones as follows:

Please make no disposition of Rice's remains until we arrive. We leave to-night, arrive New York Thursday morning.

Baker also instructed N. A. Meldrum, a Texan then in New York, to co-operate with Jones in preserving everything intact.

In the meantime, however, Swenson had notified his attorneys, who in turn had informed the police and the District Attorney's office, and that evening at about eleven o'clock James W. Gerard, accompanied by a detective, who posed as the lawyer's clerk, interviewed Patrick at his home. Patrick informed Gerard that he had an assignment of all Rice's property and also a will of Rice's of which he was executor. This was the first reference to the will of 1900. He also informed Gerard that he would not receive a cent under its provision. To have explained the real terms of the will would, under the circumstances, have excited too much suspicion. Yet he was eager to let the Swensons know that as executor he was in a position to control the profitable banking business that would arise from the settlement of the estate. In the meantime four Headquarters' detectives, representing themselves as lawyers, visited the apartments.

Patrick hurried to 500 Madison Avenue, where he learned of Meldrum's presence in town. Things were turning out far from the way in which he had expected. He then hastened to his office down-town, which he reached about half-past one in the morning, and, alone, destroyed great quantities of paper, attempting to dispose of them through the toilet bowl, which was so clogged that the water flowed out upon the floor, necessitating an apology to the janitor. In the silence of the night misgivings came upon him. He lost his nerve, and at two o'clock in the morning called up the undertaker and revoked the signed order for cremation which he had given. Leaving the office at about five in the morning he first visited Meyers, thence proceeded to his own boarding-house, and from there went to the apartments, which he reached at eight o'clock. Here he found the detectives who had been on guard since early morning to forestall any attempt to remove the body.

At the funeral itself he attempted to conciliate adverse interests and to win witnesses for his purpose. He had begun to do this the very night that Rice had died, when he told the elevator man that he was remembered in Rice's will. He had also informed Wetherbee that he had a five thousand dollars' legacy. At the funeral were Blynn, one of Rice's nephews, who had come on from Massachusetts, and two ladies, to each of whom he stated that they had legacies which would soon be available provided there was no contest of the will.

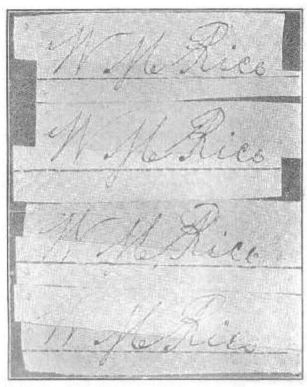

Four forged signatures of W. M. Rice, which bisected and rearranged haphazard fit exactly, thus showing that they were made from the same model. This would be an utter impossibility in the case of four genuine signatures.

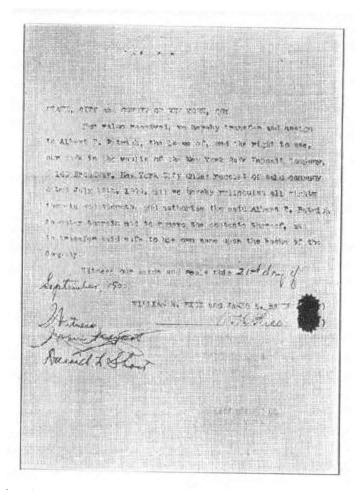

Forged assignment of vault at the New York Safe Deposit Co. from Rice to Patrick.

The detectives now informed Patrick that he was wanted at Headquarters, and Patrick invited Potts to accompany him, informing the latter that the police suspected that there was something unnatural in the cause of death, but that he could explain satisfactorily. As a matter of fact no such intimation had been made to him by the police or anyone else. At Police Headquarters after an interview with Inspector McClusky he was permitted to go his way.

Patrick returned to Rice's apartments, sent for Short and Meyers, and conferred with them there. He took this occasion to tell Maria Scott, the colored woman who worked in the apartment, that she was suspected of having poisoned Rice, and that she had better say nothing about his death. Jones told her that she was remembered in the will and that it would be worth her while to stand by himself and Patrick, who would see that she was taken care of. Meanwhile the coroner had sent the body to the morgue for autopsy.

The autopsy was performed on Tuesday, forty-three hours after death occurred, by Dr. Donlin, a coroner's physician, in the presence of Dr. Williams, also a coroner's physician, and of Professor R. A. Witthaus, an expert chemist. The two physicians testified at the trial that the organs of the body, except the lungs, were normal in condition, save as affected by the embalming fluid. They and Professor Witthaus agreed in their testimony that the lungs were congested. Dr. Donlin spoke of their being "congested all over"; while Dr. Williams characterized it as "an intense congestion of the lungs—coextensive with them." Outside of the lungs they found no evidence of disease to account for death, and beyond the congestion these showed nothing except a small patch of consolidated tissue about the size of a twenty-five cent piece. They testified, in effect, that nothing save the inhalation of some gaseous irritant could have produced such a general congestion, and that the patch of tissue referred to was insufficient to account for the amount of congestion present. Dr. Donlin could not testify what the proximate cause of death was, but was firm in his opinion that no cause for it was observable in the other vital organs. In this Dr. Williams concurred. He was of the opinion that chloroform would act as an irritant upon the lungs and cause precisely that general congestion observable in the case of the deceased. Professor Witthaus testified that his analysis revealed the presence of mercury, obtained as calomel, and while the amount was not sufficient to cause death, its presence indicated that a larger quantity had existed in life. The embalming fluid had contained no mercury, and he and Dr. Donlin agreed that the embalming fluid would have no effect upon the lungs beyond a tendency to bleach them. In other words, the People's evidence was to the effect that no cause of death was observable from a medical examination of the body save the congestion stated to exist in the lungs, and that this might have been caused by chloroform.

Thursday morning Mr. Baker and F. A. Rice, the brother of the deceased, arrived in New York. Patrick showed them the cremation letter, and, inasmuch as they took a neutral position in the matter, ordered the cremation to proceed, and accordingly it took place that very day. He also endeavored to win the confidence of Baker, but succeeded in accomplishing little. He finally gave the latter a copy of the 1900 will and the original will of 1896. He also informed Baker that he had taken a large number of papers from Rice's apartments, and turned over to him a considerable number of them. He also surrendered on Friday the two Swenson checks.

After considerable discussion Baker told Patrick flatly that he would never consent to the probate of the 1900 will; that he was satisfied that the '96 will was the last will of Rice, and that he would insist upon its being probated, to which Patrick replied, that so far as he was concerned he did not know but that the probate of the '96 will would suit him just as well as the probate of the 1900 will; that it was a matter of indifference to him, and that so far as the Rice Institute was concerned he was prepared to give Baker from three to five million dollars for it, or any other sum Baker might name. These negotiations and conferences continued until the fourth of October, Patrick yielding step by step, until he had divested himself of all control of the documents and securities.

Meantime sufficient evidence having been secured, Patrick and Jones were arrested on a charge of forgery and held for the Grand Jury. Bail was fixed at ten thousand dollars each, but was not forthcoming.

On October 21st, Mr. House, Patrick's lawyer, visited Patrick and Jones in the Tombs. Jones says that after Patrick had talked to Mr. House the former called Jones to one corner of the room and told him that House insisted on knowing definitely whether a crime had been committed and directed Jones to tell House that a murder had been committed, but that he (Patrick) was not concerned in it. This Jones declined to do without implicating Patrick. The two prisoners then returned to House and Jones says that he informed House that he had killed Rice by chloroform, and gave him the "same story which he told on the witness stand." After this Jones apparently lost his nerve and told Patrick that he intended to commit suicide. This idea Patrick encouraged, agreeing that they should both do it at about the same time.

On the 26th of October Jones made a statement to Assistant District Attorney Osborne which was in large part false, and in which he endeavored to exonerate himself entirely from complicity in any of the crimes, and in which he charged the actual administration of the chloroform to Patrick. Four days later Osborne sent for him and told him he had lied, upon which Jones became confused, continued to persist in some of his statements, qualified others and withdrew still others. He was completely unnerved and that night attempted, by means of a knife which Patrick had supplied him, to cut his throat. The attempt was a failure, and he was removed to Bellevue Hospital, where he remained until November 12th. He then finally gave the statement which corresponded with his testimony upon the trial and which jibed with all the circumstances and evidence known to the District Attorney.

Did Patrick conspire with Jones to murder Rice? What corroboration is there of Jones's story that he killed Rice under Patrick's direction? First: What proof is there that murder was committed?

Roughly, that Jones so swore; that Rice died at the time alleged; that he did not die from disease, but that he died from a congestion of the lungs which could have occurred only in the case of a living organism by the administration of some such irritant as chloroform; that some one, therefore, must have killed him, and that Jones alone had the opportunity.

Second: What proof is there that Patrick directed the murder?

Evidence of an elaborate conspiracy, as briefly heretofore set forth, which contemplated the *death* of Rice. Of course Patrick wanted Rice to die. If Patrick was not implicated in the killing, what motive had Jones to commit the deed? Why did Rice die at the precise psychological moment which would enable Patrick to prevent two hundred and fifty thousand dollars on deposit being diverted to Texas? And finally, why did Patrick prepare a forged cremation letter for the destruction of the body? If the conspiracy contemplated a *natural*death, nothing could be of greater value to the two parties concerned than the means of proving that the death was *not* unnatural.

This, in the most abbreviated form, is the case against Patrick. Space forbids any reference to his elaborate and ingenious defense, which was based entirely on an alleged complete failure of corroboration of Jones's testimony. Starting with the premise that the word of a self-confessed murderer and thrice-perjured scoundrel was valueless as proof, he contended that there was no adequate evidence that Rice's death was felonious, and that the congestion of the lungs could have been and was caused by the embalming fluid and was only attributed to the chloroform after Jones had given his final version of how the murder was accomplished. Technically the case against Patrick was not a strong one. Dramatically it was overwhelming. His own failure to testify and his refusal to allow his lawyer, Mr. House, to relate what passed between them in the Tombs, remain significant, although not evidence proper for a jury to consider. Wherever lawyers shall get together, there the Patrick case will be discussed with its strong points and its weak ones, its technicalities and its tactics, and the ethics of the liberation of Jones, the actual murderer, now long since vanished into the obscurity from which he came. On the one hand stands a public convinced of Patrick's guilt, and on the other the convicted "lifer" pointing a lean finger at the valet Jones and stubbornly repeating, "I am innocent."

[4] In 1906 the Governor of New York commuted the death sentence of Albert T. Patrick to life imprisonment, and the most extraordinary struggle in the legal history of the State on the part of a convicted murderer for his own life came to an end. The defendant in the "Death House" at Sing Sing had invoked every expedient to escape punishment, and by the use of his knowledge had even saved a fellow prisoner, "Mike" Brush, from the electric chair.

X
A Flight Into Texas

The flight and extradition of Charles F. Dodge unquestionably involved one of the most extraordinary battles with justice in the history of the criminal law. The funds at the disposal of those who were interested in procuring the prisoner's escape were unlimited in extent and the arch conspirator for whose safety Dodge was spirited away was so influential in political and criminal circles that he was all but successful in defying the prosecutor of New York County, even supported as the latter was by the military and judicial arm of the United States Government. For, at the time that Dodge made his escape, a whisper from Hummel was enough to make the dry bones of many a powerful and ostensibly respectable official rattle and the tongue cleave to the roof of his mouth in terror.

Who could accomplish that in which the law was powerless?—Hummel. Who could drive to the uttermost ends of the earth persons against whom not a shadow of suspicion had previously rested?—Hummel. Who dictated to the chiefs of police of foreign cities what they should or should not do in certain cases; and who could, at the beckoning of his little finger, summon to his dungeon-like offices in the New York Life Building, whither his firm had removed from Centre Street, the most prominent of lawyers, the most eminent of citizens?—Surely none but Hummel. And now Hummel was fighting for his own life. The only man that stood between him and the iron bars of Blackwell's Island was Charles F. Dodge—the man whom he had patted on the knee in his office and called a "Mascot," when quite in the nature of business he needed a little perjury to assist a wealthy client.

Hummel in terror called into play every resource upon which, during forty years of practice, his tiny tentacles had fastened. Who shall say that while he made a show of enjoying himself nightly with his accustomed light-heartedness in the Tenderloin, he did not feel confident that in the end this peril would disappear like the others which had from time to time threatened him during his criminal career? But Hummel was fully aware of the tenacity of the man who had resolved to rid New York of his malign influence. His Nemesis was following him. In his dreams, if he ever dreamed, it probably took the shape of the square shouldered District Attorney in the shadow of whose office building the little shyster practised his profession. Had he been told that this Nemesis was in reality a jovial little man with a round, ruddy face and twinkling blue eyes he would have laughed as heartily as it was in his power to laugh. Yet such was the fact. A little man who looked less like a detective than a commercial traveller selling St. Peter's Oil or some other cheerful concoction, with manners as gentle and a voice as soft as a spring zephyr, who always took off his hat when he came into a business office, seemingly bashful to the point of self-effacement, was the one who snatched Charles F. Dodge from the borders of Mexico and held him in an iron grip when every influence upon which Hummel could call for aid, from crooked police officials, corrupt judges and a gang of cutthroats under the guise of a sheriff's posse, were fighting for his release.

Jesse Blocher is not employed in New York County, and for business reasons he does not wish his present address known. When he comes to New York he occasionally drops into the writer's office for a cigar and a friendly chat about old times. And as he sits there and talks so modestly and with such quiet humor about his adventures with the Texas Rangers among the cactus-studded plains of the Lone Star State, it is hard even for one who knows the truth, to realize that this man is one of the greatest of detectives, or rather one of the most capable, resourceful, adroit and quick-witted knights of adventure who ever set forth upon a seemingly impossible errand.

It is unnecessary to state just how the District Attorney discovered the existence of "Jesse," as we knew him. It is enough to say that on Saturday morning, July 23, 1904, he was furnished with the proper credentials and given instructions to proceed at once to New Orleans, Louisiana, and "locate," if it were humanly possible to do so, Charles F. Dodge, under indictment for perjury, and potentially the chief witness against Abraham H. Hummel, on a charge of conspiracy. He was told briefly and to the point that, in spite of the official reports from the police head-quarters of both New York City and New Orleans to the contrary, there was reason to believe that Dodge was living, although not registered, as a guest at the St. Charles Hotel in the latter city. A partial and inaccurate description of Dodge was given him and he was warned to use extreme caution to prevent any knowledge of his mission from being made known. Once Dodge had been discovered he was to keep him under surveillance and wire New York immediately.

Accordingly, Jesse left the city upon the same day at 4.45 P.M. and arrived two days later, at 9.15 on Monday morning, at New Orleans, where he went directly to the St. Charles Hotel, registered, and was assigned to room Number 547 on the fifth floor. Somewhere in the hotel Dodge was secreted. The question was how to find him. For an hour Jesse sat in the hotel foyer and meditatively watched the visitors come and go, but saw no sign of his quarry. Then he arose, put on his hat and hunted out a stationery store where for two cents he bought a bright-red envelope. He then visited a ticket-scalper's office, secured the owner's business card and wrote a note on its back to Dodge offering him cheap transportation to any point that he might desire. Armed with this he returned to the hotel, walked to the desk, glanced casually over a number of telegrams exposed in a rack and, when the clerk turned his back, placed the note, addressed to Charles F. Dodge, unobserved, upon the counter. The office was a busy one, guests were constantly depositing their keys and receiving their mail, and, even as Jesse stood there watching developments, the clerk turned round, found the note and promptly placed it in box Number 420. The very simple scheme had worked, and quite unconsciously the clerk had indicated the number of the room occupied by Dodge.

Jesse lost no time in ascending to the fourth floor, viewed room Number 420, returned to the desk, told the clerk that he was dissatisfied with the room assigned him, and requested that he be given either room Number 421, 423, or 425, one of which he stated that he had occupied on a previous visit. After some discussion the clerk allotted him room Number 423, which was almost directly opposite that occupied by Dodge, and the detective at once took up his task of watching for the fugitive to appear.

Within the hour the door opened and Dodge and a companion, who subsequently proved to be E. M. Bracken, alias "Bradley," an agent employed by Howe and Hummel, left the room, went to the elevator and descended to the dining-room upon the second floor. Jesse watched until they were safely ensconced at breakfast and then returned to the fourth floor where he tipped the chambermaid, told her that he had left his key at the office and induced her to unlock the door of room Number 420, which she did under the supposition that Jesse was the person who had left the chamber in Dodge's company. The contents of the room convinced Jesse that he had found Dodge, for he discovered there two grips bearing Dodge's name as well as several letters on the table addressed to him. The detective returned to the hall and had a little talk with the maid.

"The old gentleman with you has been quite sick," she said. "How is he to-day?"

"He is some better," answered Jesse.

"Yes, he does look better to-day," she added, "but he sho'ly was powerful sick yesterday. Why, he hasn't been out of his room befo' fo' five or six days."

This statement was corroborated by Dodge's physical appearance, for he looked haggard and worn.

Jesse was now confident that he had found Dodge, in spite of the reports of the New Orleans police to the contrary, and he was also reasonably sure that the fugitive was too sick to leave the hotel immediately. He therefore telegraphed his superiors that he had discovered Dodge and that the latter was ill at the St. Charles Hotel.

At three o'clock in the afternoon Jesse received a wire from New York as follows:

New Orleans police department claims party not there. Left for Mexico three weeks ago. Ascertain correct destination and wire at once.

Jesse at once replied:

No question as to identity and presence here at this time.

He now took up the task of keeping his quarry under absolute surveillance day and night, which duty from that moment he continued for a period of nearly ten months.

During the remainder of the afternoon and throughout the night Dodge and Bracken remained in room Number 420, and during the evening were visited by several strangers, including a plain-clothes officer from the New Orleans Police Head-quarters. Little Hummel, dining in Long Acre Square in the glare of Broadway, was pressing some invisible button that transmitted the power of his influence even to the police government of a city two thousand miles away.

The following day, January 26th, at about 8.40 in the morning, Dodge and Bracken descended to the lobby. Bracken departed from the hotel, leaving Dodge to pay the bill at the cashier's window, and Jesse heard him order a cab for the 11.30 a.m. Sunset Limited on the Southern Pacific Railroad and direct that his baggage be removed from his room. Jesse did the same.

In the meantime Bracken returned and promptly at 11 a.m. left for the railroad station in a cab with Dodge. Jesse followed in another. As the two passed through the gates the detective caught a glimpse of Dodge's ticket and saw that it had been issued by the Mexican National Railway.

Retiring to the telegraph office in the station he wired New York as follows:

Bird flying.—Sunset Limited. Destination not known. I am with him.

He then hastily purchased a ticket to Houston, Texas, and boarded the train. Dodge's companion had bidden him good-by as the engine started, and Jesse's task now became that of ferreting out Dodge's destination. After some difficulty he managed to get a glimpse of the whole of the fugitive's ticket and thus discovered that he was on his way to the City of Mexico, via Eagle Pass, Texas, while from the Pullman conductor he learned that Dodge had secured sleeping-car accommodation as far as San Antonio, Texas, only.

So far all was well. He knew Dodge but Dodge did not know him, and later on in the afternoon he had the satisfaction of a long talk with his quarry in the observation car where they amiably discussed together current events and argued politics with the same vehemence as if they had been commercial travellers thrown fortuitously into each other's company. Dodge, however, cleverly evaded any reference to his destination.

When the train reached Morgan City, Louisiana, at 3 P.M., which was the first stop, Jesse wired New York as follows:

On Sunset Limited with friend. He has transportation to the City of Mexico, via Eagle Pass, where I am now journeying with him. Answer to Beaumont, Texas.

Later in the afternoon he sent an additional message from Lafayette, Louisiana:

Have seen transportation of friend and am positive of destination.

Dodge was occupying Section 3 of the sleeping car "Capitola," and, as became an invalid, retired early.

At Beaumont Jesse failed to receive any reply to his various messages, and when the train arrived at Houston no word came from New York until it was almost the time of departure. Waiting until practically the last moment Jesse hurried through the gates of the Union Station at Houston and bought a ticket to San Antonio. As he was leaving the ticket window Night Chief of Police John Howard and two officers came hurrying up inquiring anxiously for "Mr. Jesse." The reinforcements had arrived.

Outside on the track "The Sunset Limited" was just getting under way. The first frantic puffs were being vomited from the funnel. Inside Dodge was sleeping peacefully in his berth. Jesse, accompanied by Chief Howard, hurried up to the conductor who was about to swing on to the steps of the sleeper, and ordered him to hold the train till the fugitive could be removed. After some argument the conductor grumblingly complied and Dodge was aroused from pleasant dreams of the "Creole Quarter" to the cold reality of being dragged out of bed by a policeman. He was unceremoniously hustled out of the sleeping car into a carriage and taken to Head-quarters where he admitted his identity and remarked:

"I know what I am wanted for, but I will never return to New York."

In his grip was found the sum of $1,563.15 as well as numerous letters from the law firm of Howe and Hummel and a quantity of newspaper clippings relative to his case.

Dodge pleaded with Chief Howard not to lock him up, urging that he was a sick man and offering a goodly sum if he might be taken to a hotel and guarded for the remainder of the night. But what "went" in New Orleans, did not "go" in Houston, and the best that Dodge could get for himself was a cot in the "Ladies Detention Room" on the second floor of the jail.

Early the following morning Jesse visited Police Head-quarters and for the first time met George Ellis, Chief of Police of Houston, for whom he will always have a feeling of deep gratitude for his enthusiastic cooperation and loyalty in the many stirring events that followed. Dodge now received a telegram from New York, which was submitted to Jesse before reaching the prisoner, to the effect that Howe and Hummel were sending on an attorney to aid the fugitive in resisting extradition, and informing him that they had employed Messrs. Hunt and Meyers as attorneys to look out for his welfare. These last immediately jumped *in medias res* and on the afternoon of the same day secured a writ of habeas corpus from Norman J. Kitrell, District Judge of Harris County, Texas, returnable the following morning.

The next day, January 28th, Kitrell released Dodge from custody.

Jesse had anticipated this and immediately swore out another warrant with the result that the prisoner was rearrested before he left the court room.

Meantime the Dodge interests retained another firm of lawyers, Messrs. Andrews and Ball, who, on the following day, secured a second writ of habeas corpus from Judge Ashe.

The result of the first engagement thus being a draw, counsel on both sides agreed that this writ should not be returnable for six days. During this period District Attorney Jerome employed Messrs. Baker Botts, Parker and Garwood to represent him and secured from Governor Odell at Albany a requisition on Governor Lanham of Texas for the extradition of the prisoner, which he entrusted to Detective Sergeant Herlihy of the New York Police. Herlihy reached Houston with the papers on the evening of January 30th, and on the same train with him came Abraham Kaffenburgh, a member of the law firm of Howe and Hummel and a nephew of the latter. Likewise also came Bracken, still styling himself "E. M. Bradley," and from now on Bracken was the inseparable companion, guide, philosopher and friend (?) of the unfortunate Dodge whose continued existence upon this earth had become such a menace to the little lawyer in New York.

Herlihy, accompanied by Judge Garwood, proceeded direct to Austin where they found Dodge already represented by Messrs. Andrews and Ball who, at the hearing before Governor Lanham, made a strong effort to induce that executive to refuse to honor the requisition of the Governor of New York. This effort failed and Governor Lanham issued his warrant, but Herlihy had no sooner returned to Houston for the purpose of taking possession of the prisoner than he was served with an injunction enjoining him, together with Chief of Police Ellis, from taking Dodge into custody, pending a hearing upon a new habeas corpus which had been issued by Judge Waller T. Burns of the United States District Court for the Southern District of Texas. This new writ was returnable February 9th.

After exhaustive but futile argument by the counsel for Dodge, Judge Burns remanded the prisoner to Herlihy's custody to be returned to the State of New York, but this decision had no sooner been rendered than an appeal was taken therefrom by Dodge's lawyers, and the prisoner released upon bail fixed at twenty thousand dollars.

During this period Dodge was quartered under guard at the Rice Hotel in Houston, and the day following the argument the twenty-thousand-dollars bail was put up in cash and Dodge released from custody.

In the meantime, however, Jesse, knowing that no sum, however large, would deter Hummel from spiriting Dodge out of the country, had made his arrangements to secure a new extradition warrant from the Governor of Texas, so that if the prisoner did succeed in getting beyond the Southern District of the Federal Court of Texas, he could be seized and conveyed to New York.

Of course some one had to keep watch over Dodge while Jesse hurried to Austin to see the Governor, and it was decided to leave Sergeant Herlihy, reinforced by a number of local detectives for that purpose. But while the watchful Jesse was away, Bracken proceeded to get busy in the good old Howe and Hummel fashion. Lots of people that Herlihy had never seen before turned up and protested that he was the finest fellow they had ever met. And as Herlihy was, in fact, a good fellow, he made them welcome and dined and wined at their expense until he woke up in the Menger Hotel in San Antonio and inquired where he was.

Jesse meantime had returned from Austin to discover that Dodge with his companions, Kaffenburgh and Bracken, had slipped out of Houston early in the morning of February 11th, after disposing of Herlihy and eluding the watchfulness of Herlihy's assistants. Hummel was leading and by ten o'clock the next morning Dodge and his comrades were on board an English merchantman lying in the harbor of Galveston. Later in the same day the Hummel interests chartered from the Southern Pacific Railroad for the sum of three thousand dollars the sea-going tug *Hughes*, to which Dodge was now transferred for the purpose of being conveyed to the port of Tampico in the Republic of Mexico.

But here Hummel's wires became crossed with Jerome's, and unfortunately for the little lawyer, the persons from whom the tug had been leased turned out to be closely allied with the prosecution's interests, with the result that the captain of the tug was instructed by his superiors under no consideration to put into any Mexican port, but on the contrary, to delay his departure from the harbor of Galveston for a period of two days and then to proceed only as far as Brownsville, Texas, where he should compel the debarkation of the fugitive. The captain, who was a good sport as well as a good officer, promptly threw himself into the part and told Bracken and Kaffenburgh that it was evident from the barometer that a severe storm was approaching (which must have had a sinister implication to these two unfortunate gentlemen), and that he could not think of putting to sea. Once the "storm" had blown over, the tug started out across the blue waters of the Gulf of Mexico. But now Bracken and Kaffenburgh were informed for the first time that it was impossible to consider putting into any port of the Republic of Mexico, since to do so would cause international complications and compel the revocation of the captain's license. In desperation the Hummel interests offered the captain five thousand dollars in cash to disregard his instructions and put into Tampico, but the worthy sea-dog was adamant. It was probably worth five thousand dollars to him to see three gentry of this pattern so much put about.

While Dodge and his accomplices were dallying in the harbor of Galveston, Jesse was taking advantage of his opportunity to proceed at once by railroad to Alice, Texas, which at that time was the furthermost southern point reached by any railway in the direction of Brownsville. On his arrival, he at once applied to Captain John R. Hughes, commanding Company D of the Texas Rangers, who received him with great joy and ordered a detachment of the Rangers to meet the tug at Point Isabella at the mouth of the Rio Grande River on the border of Mexico. In the meantime, Jesse started on a toilsome stage journey to Brownsville, across one hundred and seventy miles of desert, which occupied two days and nights, and necessitated his going without sleep for that period. During the trip Jesse heard no word of English and had as his associates only Mexican cattlemen. Every fifteen miles a fresh relay of broncos was hitched to the stage and after a few moments' rest the misery began again.

Jesse had been hurrying toward Brownsville by stage while Dodge, Kaffenburgh and Bracken were landing at Point Isabella, where they were kept under close surveillance by Sergeant Tom Ross of the Rangers. Thence they took the train to Brownsville, registering at the Miller House under the assumed names of C. F. Dougherty, A. Koontzman and E. M. Barker, all of Oklahoma. But, although they knew it not, Sergeant Tom was at their elbow, and had Dodge attempted to cross the border into Mexico he would instantly have been placed under arrest.

As Brownsville was within the Southern District of the Federal Court of Texas, Jesse decided not to arrest Dodge until he should actually attempt flight, and when Dodge and his companions, on the following morning, February 15th, entered the stage (the same upon which Jesse had arrived) and started for Alice, Jesse and Tom Ross procured the best horses they could find and started after them, keeping just in sight of the stage. Dodge's intention in making this move was to take the Mexican International Railway at Alice and cross over to Mexico via Laredo.

Jesse and Ross covered the seventy-four miles from Brownsville to Santa La Cruz Ranch by four in the afternoon, which was fairly strenuous work for a New York detective, and here found themselves so sore and exhausted from their ride that they were glad to hire a pair of horses and buggy with which to complete the journey to Alice. Luckily they were able to get into telephonic communication with various ranch owners along the road and arrange to have fresh relays of horses supplied to them every twenty miles, and here also Jesse called up Captain Hughes at Alice, and suggested that he substitute for the regular night clerk at the City Hotel one of the privates of the Rangers by the name of Harrod.

Dodge and his companions arrived in Alice on February 17th, and, as Jesse had anticipated, repaired at once to the City Hotel, where, inasmuch as they were dry from the dust of their trip and depressed by lack of society, they entered at once into an enthusiastic and confidential friendship with the man behind the counter in the hotel office, sublimely ignorant that they were unfolding to a member of the Texas Rangers all their most secret intentions. Harrod was just as glad to see Dodge as Dodge apparently was to see Harrod, and kindly offered to assist the fugitive to get into Mexico in any way that the latter desired. Dodge, for his part, took advantage of his usefulness to the extent of requesting him to purchase them railroad tickets, the plan being to leave Alice the following morning for Monterey, Mexico. Three hours after the stage bearing Dodge and his party pulled up at the City Hotel, Tom Ross and Jesse drove in behind a pair of fagged-out broncos at two in the morning. Jesse had had no sleep of any sort and no proper nourishment for five days, and had just strength enough left to drag himself up one flight of stairs and tumble into bed, from which he did not emerge for many hours.

In the meantime day broke and Dodge, Kaffenburgh and Bracken, having breakfasted, drove comfortably down to the International Railway Station and settled themselves in the smoker, but they had no sooner given this direct evidence of their intention before Captain Hughes entered and placed Dodge under arrest. The latter's surprise may be appreciated when it is stated that from the time the three had left Houston, they had no idea that they were being followed and believed that they had completely foiled Jesse and his assistants.

While Jesse had been chasing Dodge across the desert, his lawyers had not been idle and had secured at Austin another extradition warrant from Governor Lanham, who, on receiving news of the arrest, promptly instructed Captain Hughes by wire to assume charge of the prisoner and to deliver him into the hands of the New York officer to be conveyed to New York.

There now began such a legal battle as the State of Texas had never known. Hummel had been forced into his last ditch and was fighting desperately for life. Through Kaffenburgh he at once applied for a new writ of habeas corpus in Nueces County and engaged counsel at Corpus Christie to assist in fighting for the release of the prisoner. Precisely as Hummel had intended, Chief Wright of Nueces rode into Alice and demanded the prisoner from Captain Hughes. As Hummel had *not* intended, Captain Hughes refused to surrender the prisoner and told Chief Wright to go to—well, he told him that he intended to obey his commander-in-chief, the Governor of Texas.

On February 20th, Hummel, through Kaffenburgh, attempted to get another writ of habeas corpus in Bee County, and promptly the Bee chief came buzzing over and demanded Dodge, but to him Hughes replied even as he had spoken to Wright.

Excitement in Alice had now reached such a pitch that Judge Burns, of the Federal Court, in Houston, ordered United States Marshal John W. Vann, of Alice, to assume charge of the prisoner. The indomitable Hughes, however, paid no more attention to the United States Marshal than he had to the local chiefs. But the situation was so delicate and the clash of authority might so easily have resulted in bloodshed that it was finally agreed by all parties that the best thing to do was to have the prisoner returned to Houston in the *joint* custody of Captain Hughes of the Rangers and the United States Marshal.

Jesse, through his counsel, in proper course made application to forfeit Dodge's bond and remand him to jail, but the Hummel attorneys finally induced the Court, on the plea that to confine Dodge in jail would be detrimental to his already badly impaired health, to permit the prisoner to go free on a greatly increased bond, nevertheless restricting his movements to Harris County, Texas.

While Jesse had fought a winning battle up to this point he was at the end of his resources so far as the extradition of the prisoner was concerned, for Dodge was now at liberty, pending the decisions upon the habeas corpus proceedings of the United States Circuit Court of Appeals at Fort Worth, and the United States Supreme Court at Washington. But his orders were to *bring Dodge back to* New York. Hence, with the aid of some new men sent him from the North, he commenced an even closer surveillance of the prisoner than ever before by both day and night.

Meantime Kaffenburgh departed for New York, fleeing from the wrath of Judge Burns, who had issued a summons for him for contempt of the Federal Court on the ground that he had induced Dodge to attempt to jump his bond. In place of the blustering Kaffenburgh was sent another member of the famous law firm of Howe and Hummel, David May, an entirely different type of man. May was as mild as a day in June—as urbane as Kaffenburgh had been insolent. He fluttered into Houston like a white dove of peace with the proverbial olive branch in his mouth. From now on the tactics employed by the representatives of Hummel were conciliatory in the extreme. Mr. May, however, did not long remain in Houston, as it was apparent that there was nothing to be done by either side pending the action of the courts, and in any event Dodge was abundantly supplied with local counsel. The time had now come when Hummel must have begun to feel that the fates were against him and that a twenty-year term in state prison was a concrete possibility even for him.

In the meantime, Dodge and Bracken had taken up their headquarters at the Rice Hotel in the most expensive suite of rooms in the house, a new scheme for getting the prisoner beyond the reach of the New York courts apparently having been concocted. Dodge was now indulged in every conceivable luxury and vice. He was plunged into every sort of excess, there was no debauchery which Bracken could supply that was not his and their rapid method of existence was soon the talk of the county and continued to be so for ten long months. There is more than one way to kill a cat and more than one method of wiping out the only existing witness against a desperate man striving to escape the consequences of crime.

Dodge's daily routine was somewhat as follows: He never slept at his own hotel, but arose in the morning between ten and eleven o'clock, when he was at once visited by Bracken and supplied with numerous drinks in lieu of the breakfast for which he never had any desire. At noon the two would have luncheon with more drinks. In the afternoon they would retire to the pool rooms and play the races, and, when the races were over, they would then visit the faro banks and gamble until midnight or later. Later on they would proceed to another resort on Louisiana Street where Dodge really lived. Here his day may be said to have begun and here he spent most of his money, frequently paying out as much as fifty dollars a night for wine and invariably ending in a beastly state of intoxication. It is quite probable that never in the history of debauchery has any one man ever been so indulged in excesses of every sort for the same period of time as Dodge was during the summer and fall of 1904. The fugitive never placed his foot on mother earth. If they were going only a block, Bracken called for a cab, and the two seemed to take a special delight in making Jesse, as Jerome's representative, spend as much money in cab hire as possible. The Houston jehus never again experienced so profitable a time as they did during Dodge's wet season; and the life of dissipation was continued until, from time to time, the prisoner became so weak from its effects that he was forced to go under the care of a physician. A few days of abstinence always restored his vitality and he would then start out upon another round of pleasure.

During this period Jesse maintained a close and vigilant personal espionage over the prisoner. For over ten months he slept less than four hours each day, his fatigue being increased by the constant apprehension of treachery among his own men, and the necessity of being ever on the alert to prevent some move on the part of the defense to spirit the prisoner away. During the summer attempts were repeatedly made to evade the vigilance of Jesse and his men and several desperate dashes were frustrated by them, including one occasion when Bracken succeeded in rushing Dodge as far as Galveston, where they were forced to abandon their design.

From time to time Bracken would disappear from Houston for a week or ten days, stating on his return that he had been to New York, after which there was invariably some new move to get the prisoner away. Time and space prevent giving a detailed account of all the marches and counter-marches that took place in this battle of wit against wit.

In August, 1904, Bracken made one of his periodical visits to New York, and when he returned sought out Jesse and said: "Blocher, you might as well be a good fellow and get yours while you can. I mean that Dodge is not going back to New York, even if it cost a million dollars to prevent it." A few days later Bracken sent a gambler named Warner to Jesse, who offered the latter thirty-five hundred dollars to get "lost" long enough for the prisoner to slip over to Mexico. Acting upon the advice of his attorney, Jesse encouraged this attempt, under the belief that if he could get the Hummel forces in the position of having attempted to bribe him the prisoner's bail could then be forfeited and Dodge himself taken into custody. Hummel became wary, however, and apparently abandoned for the time the idea of bribery. Later on Bracken again disappeared. On his return a marked change was noticeable in his demeanor and Jesse observed that he was in constant consultation with Dodge, from which the detective drew the inference that some last desperate move was to be made towards the escape of the prisoner.

On one occasion Jesse saw Bracken showing Dodge a map and some drawings on paper, which so excited his suspicions that he followed the two with unremitting assiduity, and within a day or two was rewarded through Bracken's carelessness with an opportunity for going through the latter's coat pockets in the billiard room. Here he found a complete set of plans worked out in every detail for spiriting the prisoner from San Antonio into Mexico during the State Fair. These plans were very elaborate, every item having been planned out from the purchase of tickets, and passing of baggage through the customs, to hotel accommodation in the City of Mexico and Tampico, and steamship tickets from Tampico to Europe.

The plan had been to secure permission from the Court for Dodge to leave Houston long enough ostensibly to attend the Fair at San Antonio and to "lose" him during the excitement and crowded condition of the city at that time.

It is, of course, needless to say that these plans were abandoned when Bracken discovered that Jesse had been forewarned.

Almost immediately thereafter the Circuit Court of Appeals at Fort Worth, Texas, decided one of the habeas corpus cases adversely to Dodge but it still permitted him to retain his liberty pending the final determination of the questions involved by the Supreme Court at Washington.

The Hummel forces were apparently losing hope, however, for early in October another attempt was made to bribe Jesse. Bracken entered his room one evening and informed him that he could get his own price if he would only be a good fellow, and even went so far as to exhibit a quantity of money which he stated was twenty-five thousand dollars. The only result of this offer was to lead Jesse to redouble his precautions, for he argued that the situation must indeed be acute when such an offer could be deemed worth while. Thereafter it was obvious that the revelry of Dodge and his companions was on the increase. Accordingly Jesse added to his force of assistants.

On December 2, 1904, Nathaniel Cohen, another member of the firm of Howe and Hummel, arrived at Houston, and the next day the Supreme Court at Washington decided the appeal in the habeas corpus against the prisoner, who was at once ordered by Judge Burns into the custody of United States Marshal William M. Hanson.

Things looked black indeed for Dodge and blacker still for Hummel. How the little attorney, eating his midday lunch four thousand miles away, at Pontin's restaurant on Franklin Street, must have trembled in his patent leather boots! His last emissary, Cohen, at once procured an assistant by the name of Brookman and with him proceeded to Wharton County, Texas, where they secured a new writ of habeas corpus and induced the local sheriff, one Rich, to swear in a *posse comitatus* of one hundred men for the purpose of coming to Houston to take the prisoner by force of arms out of the hands of the United States Marshal.

This was one of the most daring and desperate attempts made in recent years to frustrate the law. Jesse believes that the real object of this *posse* was to precipitate a fight between themselves and the Federal authorities. It is not inconceivable that in such an event Dodge might either have escaped or been killed. The men composing the *posse* were of the most desperate character, and consisted largely of the so-called "feud factions" of Wharton County, known as "The Wood Peckers" and "The Jay Birds." Jesse has been informed, on what he regards as reliable authority, that this move cost the Hummel forces fifteen thousand dollars and that each member of the *posse* received one hundred dollars for his contemplated services in the "rescue" of the prisoner. But civil war, even on a small scale, cannot be indulged in without some inkling of the facts becoming known to the authorities, and prior to the receipt of the mandate of the Supreme Court, Judge Burns ordered the prisoner removed to Galveston for safe keeping.

Thus the long, expensive and arduous struggle came finally to an end, for Judge Burns in due course, ordered that Charles F. Dodge should be conveyed to New York in the personal custody of the United States Marshal and delivered by him to the New York authorities "within the borders of that State." Such an order was, of course, exceedingly unusual, if not almost unheard of, but it was rendered absolutely necessary by the powerful influence and resources, as well as the unscrupulous character, of those interested in securing Dodge's disappearance.

In order to thwart any plans for releasing the prisoner by violence or otherwise, and to prevent delay through the invoking of legal technicalities, Hansen and Jesse decided to convey Dodge to New York by water, and on the 16th of December, the Marshal and his five deputies boarded a Mallory Line steamer at Galveston and arrived in New York with their prisoner on the evening of December 23d.

Dodge reached New York a physical wreck. How he was induced to tell the whole truth after he had pleaded guilty to the charge against him is a story in itself. A complete reaction from his dissipation now occurred and for days his life was despaired of. Jesse, too, was, as the expression is, "all in," and the only persons who were still able to appreciate the delights of New York were the stalwart Marshal and his boys, who for some time were objects of interest as they strolled along Broadway and drank "deep and hearty" in the cafés. To the assistants in the District Attorney's office they were heroes and were treated as such.

How Dodge finally testified against Hummel on the witness stand has already been told. As they say down-town, if Jerome had never done anything else, he would have "made good" by locking up Abe Hummel. No one ever believed he would do it. But Jerome never would have locked up Hummel without Jesse. And, as Jesse says with a laugh, leaning back in his chair and taking a long pull on his cigar, "I guess I would not do it again—no, I *would* not do it again for all the money you could give me. The wonder is that I came out of it alive." When the reader comes to think about it he will probably agree with him.

XI
A Case of Circumstantial Evidence

In the town of Culiano, in the province of Salano, in Italy, there dwelt a widow by the name of Torsielli, with her two sons, Vito and Antonio. The boys loved their mother devotedly and were no less fond of each other, the height of their ambition being to earn enough money to support her in comfort without need of working in her old age. As it was, she arose before light, made the fire, cooked their breakfast and labored in and about the house all day until they returned from the fields. But she was getting old and at last became bedridden and infirm. She could no longer cook the meals, and the boys had to shift for themselves. Moreover, instead of finding her standing at the door with a smile on her wrinkled face, welcoming them to supper on their return, the fire was always out and their mother lay on her couch, no less glad to see them, to be sure, but no longer able to amuse them or minister to their comfort. Then the taxes were increased and hard times came. By twos and threes the men of the village packed their bundles, bade good-by to their friends and families, and left the town, some to seek work in other parts of Italy, but most of them to take the big iron steamships for America, where work was easy and money plentiful. Sadly the boys watched their comrades depart. They would have liked to go, too, to seek their fortunes in this new land of promise, but they could not leave their mother. The following year some of the men who had gone away to America returned in fine clothes and with full purses to tell of the wonderful country beyond the seas, where one could always earn his ten *lire* every day and do as he liked. "Viva la liberta!" they cried, pounding the tables in the café. "Come, comrades! We have plenty of money. Drink to the great country of America!"

Vito and Antonio listened with envy. One evening the elder brother asked Antonio to come to walk with him. When they had gone a little way he said suddenly:

"Toni, I think I shall go to this America. We need more money to make our mother comfortable. If we wait until she is dead the money will be of no use. You can stay here, and when I have made a place for you and her, you shall bring her on the ship to the new country."

Vito was five years older than Antonio, and his word had always been law to the younger brother, so although he was sick at heart at the thought of being left behind, he said nothing against the project, but tried to make it easy for Vito with their mother. The old woman could not bear the thought of her firstborn leaving her, and declared, with the tears running down her face, that she should never see him again, but at last she yielded to their persuasions and gave Vito her blessing. It would be only a little while before she and Toni would join him, and they would be happy ever after.

Then Toni was left alone with his mother. Every day he arose at the first streak of dawn, prepared breakfast, cleaned the house, saw that his mother was comfortable and then started off for the fields. A month went by, two months, three, a year, but no word came from Vito. Toni assured the poor old woman that they would certainly hear from him the next week or the next, but cruel fear had taken possession of him. Something had happened to his brother! The years swept on. Their mother became more and more helpless. Antonio was obliged to hire a woman to care for her as nurse for a small sum, but it was just enough to leave only a pittance for them to live on. Toni grew thin and haggard. Where could Vito be? Was he alive or dead? Next to his love for Nicoletta Lupero it became the great passion of his life to learn what had become of Vito.

He had known Nicoletta from a child and their love had followed as naturally as summer follows spring. It had always been "Toni" and "Nicoletta" ever since he could remember. But she was growing up, and from a boy he had become a man. Yet how could he marry when he could hardly earn enough to support his mother and himself? They talked it over time and time again. If Vito would only return or good times come it might be possible. But meantime there was nothing to do but wait. Nicoletta blossomed into womanhood. Had she not been betrothed she would have been called an old maid. Neither she nor Toni took any part in the village merrymakings. Why should they? He was thirty and she twenty-five. They might have married ten years ago had not the elder brother gone away. Toni secretly feared that the time would never come when they would be man and wife, but he patiently labored on earning his two *lire*, or at most two *lire* and a half, a day.

Then a man returned from America just for the harvest to see his family. He said that Vito was alive. He had not seen him himself, but others had seen him and he was rich. He told of the plentifulness of gold in America, where every one was comfortable and could lay up a fortune. He himself had saved over five thousand *lire* in four years and owned a one-third interest in a fruit store. He was going to take his brother's family back with him—all of them. They would be rich, too, in a little while. A man was a fool to stay in Italy. Why did not Toni come back with him? He would get him a place on the railroad where one of his friends was padrone.

Toni discussed it all with Nicoletta, and she talked with the man herself.

"Toni," she said at length, "why do you not go? Here you are earning nothing. There you could save in a month enough to keep your mother in comfort for a year. You have to pay the nurse, and that takes a great deal. While you are here it would cause talk if I came to live in your home to care for your mother but if you go away I can do so without comment and it will cost nothing. Perhaps you will find Vito. If not you will soon make enough to send for both your mother and me."

"You are a good girl," he answered, kissing her, "but I could not shift the responsibility of my mother to your shoulders. Still, I will talk to Father Giuseppi about it."

The priest thought well of the plan (he was a little excited over America himself), and agreed to break the matter to the mother.

She begged Toni piteously not to go. He was her only surviving son. Vito was dead. Let him but wait a little while and she would not be there to stand in his way. Then the priest added his personal assurance that it would be for the best, and the mother finally gave way. Toni was obliged to tear himself away by force from the arms of the old woman lying upon the bed, and her feeble sobs echoed in his ears as he trudged down the road with the scarf Nicoletta had worked about his neck, and a small bundle of his tools and most precious possessions on his shoulder. A couple of miles farther on came another harrowing parting with his betrothed, and from the top of the next rise beyond he could see Nicoletta still standing at the crossroads gazing pitifully after him. Thus many an Italian, for good or ill, has left the place of his birth for the mysterious land of the Golden West.

The voyage was for Antonio an unalloyed agony of seasickness and homesickness, and when at last the great vessel steamed slowly up the North River, her band playing and the emigrants crowding eagerly to her sides, he had hardly spirit enough left to raise his eyes to the mountains of huge buildings from whose craters the white smoke rose slowly and blew away in great wind-torn clouds. Yet he felt some of the awakening enthusiasm of his comrades, and when once his feet touched earth again it was not long before he almost forgot his sufferings upon the ocean in his feverish anxiety to lose no time in beginning to save the money which should reunite him to Nicoletta and his mother. As soon as the vessel had docked a blustering Italian came among the emigrants and tagged a few dozen of them, including Antonio, with large blue labels, and then led them in a long, straggling line across the gangplank and marched them through the muddy streets to the railroad train. Here they huddled in a dirty car filled with smoke and were whirled with frightful speed for hours through a flat and smiling country. The noise, the smoke and the unaccustomed motion made Antonio ill again, and when the train stopped at Lambertville, New Jersey, the padrone had difficulty in rousing him from the animal-like stupor into which he had fallen.

The Italians crowded together upon the platform, gazing helplessly at one another and at the padrone, who was cursing them for a lot of stupid fools, and bidding them get upon a flat car that stood upon a siding. Antonio had to be pushed upon it by main force, but the journey this time was short, and in half an hour he found himself upon an embankment where hundreds of Italians were laboring with pick and shovel in the broiling sun. Here he also was given a pick and told to go to work.

Toni soon became accustomed to his new surroundings. Every night he and the rest were carried to Lambertville on flat cars and in the mornings were brought back to the embankment. The work was no harder than that to which he had been used, and he soon became himself again. Moreover, he found many of his old friends from Culiano working there. In the evenings they walked through the streets of the town or sat under the trees playing *mora* and *tocco*. His letters home were quite enthusiastic regarding the pleasant character of the life. To be sure he could not write himself, but his old friend Antonio Strollo, who had lived at Valva, only a mile from Culiano, acted as his amanuensis. He was very fond of Strollo, who was a dashing fellow, very merry and quite the beau of the colony, in his wonderful red socks and neckties of many colors. Strollo could read and write, and, besides, he knew Antonio's mother and Nicoletta, and when Toni found himself unable to express his thoughts Strollo helped him out. When the answers came he read them to Toni and joined in the latter's pleasure. Toni himself soon became a favorite in Lambertville, for he was simple and gentle, and full of good-will for everybody. He was very good-looking, too, with his handsome Roman profile, snapping black eyes and black curly locks. Yet he was sad always, especially so as since his arrival in America he had made no progress toward finding Vito. From time to time he met other Italians who had been working elsewhere, who thought they had seen him or some one that looked like him. But inquiry always elicited the fact that their desire to give him encouragement was greater than the accuracy of their memories. Of course Antonio Strollo, who had become Toni's inseparable friend, shared all his eagerness to find Vito. In fact, Toni had no thought that he did not confide to his friend, and it was really the latter who composed the love letters to Nicoletta and the affectionate epistles to the mother.

Every month Toni divided what he earned into three parts. One of them he deposited in the savings-bank, another he invested in a money order which was sent by Strollo to Nicoletta for the mother, and the last he kept for himself. It was astounding how fast one really could make money if one was industrious. Forty dollars a month, sometimes! That made nearly seventy *lire* to send to Nicoletta. His bank account grew steadily, and he often saved something out of the money he allowed himself to live upon.

Antonio Strollo, on the other hand, was lazy and spent all his wages on *chianti*, neckties, waistcoats, and gambling. Sometimes he would do nothing for a whole month but loiter around the streets smoking cigars and ogling the village girls. These last were afraid of him and called him "The Dare Devil."

Toni worked on the embankment for three years, sending his money with a letter to Nicoletta every month. The mother still lived and Nicoletta was giving up her own life to take care of her, but the old woman was very feeble and no longer had any hope of seeing either of her sons again. Moreover, she was now so bedridden that it was useless to think of trying to move her, even if Toni had plenty of money. No, as soon as he was satisfied that Vito could not be found and had saved enough money he must return. How she begged him to return! As Strollo read him the girl's letters Toni wept bitter tears and Strollo wept likewise in sympathy. But no word came of Vito.

Toni, anxious about his mother, despairing of ever finding his brother, pining for Nicoletta and with three hundred dollars lying in the savings-bank, decided to return to Italy. But if only he could find Vito first! Then Antonio Strollo had an idea. Why not advertise, he suggested. He wondered that they had never thought of it before. They would put a notice in *Il Progresso*, the Italian paper in New York, and see what would come of it. Toni agreed that the idea was good, so Strollo wrote the notice offering a reward for news of Vito.

Two months passed, once more Toni gave up hope, and then, O-never-to-be-forgotten day! a letter came from the post-office from Vito! Toni threw his arms about Strollo and kissed him for joy. Vito was found at last! The letter, dated Yonkers, New York, told how Vito had by chance heard of Toni's notice and learned that he was in America. He himself, he said, had prospered and was a padrone, employing many workmen on the water-works. He begged Toni for news of their mother. He confessed himself an ungrateful son never to have written, but he had married and had had children, and he had assumed that she was being cared for by his brother. Toni must forgive him and come to him at once.

"O Dio!" cried Toni, the tears in his eyes. "Forgive him? Of course I will forgive him! Come, Antonio, let us write my dear brother a letter without delay and tell him that our mother is still alive. How should I like to see his wife and babies!"

So they prepared a long letter which Strollo took to the post-office himself and mailed. Toni went back to work with joy in his heart and whistled and sang all day long, and, of course, he wrote all about it to Nicoletta. He was only waiting for his month to be up before starting. Then he would go to Yonkers, make Vito a little visit, and return home to Italy. It would be easy enough, after that, for Vito would send them money, if necessary, to live upon.

Several letters passed between the brothers, and at the end of the month Toni drew out his money from the bank, received his wages in full, and prepared to leave Lambertville. Meantime a letter had come from Nicoletta telling of his mother's joy at learning that Vito was still alive.

As Toni had doubts as to his ability to find his way to Yonkers, Strollo kindly offered to accompany him. Toni had made many friends during his three-years' stay in Lambertville, and he promised to write to them and tell them about Vito and his family, so it was agreed that the letter should be sent to Sabbatto Gizzi, in whose house he had lived, and that Gizzi should read it to the others. The address was written carefully on a piece of paper and given to Toni.

So early in the morning of August 16th, 1903, Toni and Strollo took the train for New York. It was a hot day, and once again the motion and speed made Toni feel ill, but the thought of seeing Vito buoyed him up, and by the time they had crossed the ferry and had actually reached New York he was very hungry. In his excitement he had forgotten to eat any breakfast and was now beginning to feel faint. But Strollo said it was a long way to Yonkers and that they must not stop. For many hours they trudged the streets without getting anywhere and then Strollo said it was time to take the cars. Toni was very tired, and he had to climb many flights of stairs to the train. It carried them a long distance, past miles of tenement houses and vacant lots, and at last into a sort of country. Strollo said they should get out. It was very hot and Toni was weak from weariness and lack of food, but his heart was light and he followed Strollo steadily down the wilting road. After going about a mile they crossed some fields near where people were playing a game at hitting little balls with sticks. It was astonishing how far they could strike the balls—entirely out of sight.

"Is this Yonkers?" asked Toni.

"It is near here," answered Strollo. "We are going by a short way."

They entered some thick woods and came out upon another field. Toni was now so faint that he begged his friend to stop.

"Can we not get some food?" he inquired; "I can hardly walk."

"There is a man in that field," said Strollo. "Go and ask him."

So Toni plodded over to the man who was digging mushrooms and asked him in broken English where they could get something to eat. The man told him that it was a long way. They would have to take the trolley to Yonkers. There was a restaurant there called the "Promised Land," where one could get Italian dishes. He seemed to take a kindly interest in Toni and in Strollo, who had remained some distance behind, and Toni gave him a cigar—a "Cremo"—the last one he had. Then Strollo led the way back into the woods.

It was almost sunset, and the long, low beams slanting through the tree trunks made it hard to see. They went deeper and deeper into the woods. Presently Strollo, who was leading the way, stopped and said:

"We are going in the wrong direction. We must turn around and go back."

Toni turned. As he did so Strollo drew a long knife and plunged it again and again through Toni's body.

Strollo spent that night, under an assumed name, at the Mills Hotel in Bleecker Street. He had stabbed himself accidentally in the knee and also in the left hand in the fury of his attack, and when he arose in the morning the sheets were covered with blood. There was also blood on his shoes, which had been new, but he took his knife and scraped it off. He had experienced a strange sort of terrified exaltation the night before, and in the early light as he crept downstairs and out of the hotel he could not have told whether he were more glad or afraid. For he had three hundred dollars in his pocket, more than he had ever seen at any one time before—as much as a man could save in two whole years. He would be a king now for a long time. He need not work. He could eat, drink and play cards and read some books he had heard about. As for finding him out—never! The police would not even know who Torsielli was, to say nothing of who had killed him, for he had removed, as he thought, everything in Toni's pockets. There would be a dead man in the morgue, that was all. He could go back to Lambertville and say that he had left Toni with his brother, at Yonkers, and that would be the end of it. First, though, he would buy some new clothes.

It was very early and the shops were hardly open, but he found one place where he could buy a suit, another some underclothes, and a third a pair of shoes. The shoemaker, who was a thrifty man, asked Strollo what was the matter with the shoes he had on, so Strollo craftily said they hurt his feet. Then he ate a hearty breakfast, and bought a better cigar than he had ever smoked before. There was a bookstore near by and he purchased some books—"Alto Amore" and "Sua Maestá e Sua Moneta" ("The Height of Love" and "His Majesty and His Money"). He would read them on the train. He felt warm and comfortable now and not afraid at all. By and by he went back on the train to Lambertville and smoked and read all the way, contented as the tiger is contented which has tracked down and slain a water-buffalo.

The same afternoon about sunset, in a lonely part of Van Cortlandt Park, the mushroom digger stumbled over Torsielli's body lying face downward among the leaves. He recognized it as that of the man who had asked the way to something to eat and given him a cigar. He ran from the sight and, pallid with fear, notified the nearest police officer. Then things took the usual course. The body was removed to the morgue, an autopsy was performed, and "Headquarters" took charge of the case. As the deceased was an Italian, Detective Sergeant Petrosini was called in. Torsielli's pockets were empty save for the band of a "Cremo" cigar in one waistcoat pocket and a tiny slip of paper in another, on which was penciled "Sabbatto Gizzi, P.O. Box 239, Lambertville, New Jersey." Whether this last was the name of the deceased, the murderer, or some one else, no one knew. Headquarters said it was a blind case, but Petrosini shrugged his shoulders and bought a ticket to Lambertville.

Here he found Sabbatto Gizzi, who expressed genuine horror at learning of Toni's death and readily accompanied Petrosini to New York, where he identified the body as indeed that of Torsielli. He told Petrosini that Toni had left Lambertville in the company of Strollo on Thursday, August 16th. This was Saturday, August 18th, and less than thirty-six hours after the murder. Strollo, reading "Alto Amore," and drinking in the saloon, suspected nothing. New York was seventy miles away—too far for any harm to come. But Monday morning, walking lazily down the street near the railroad station, Strollo found himself suddenly confronted by a heavily-built man with a round, moon-shaped face thickly covered with pockmarks. Strollo did not like the way the latter's gimlet-like eyes looked him over. There was no time to turn and fly, and, besides, Strollo had no fear. They might come and ask him questions, and he might even admit almost all—*almost* all, and they could do nothing, for no one had seen what he had done to Toni in the wood. So Strollo returned Petrosini's gaze unflinchingly.

"Are you Antonio Strollo?" asked the detective, coming close to the murderer.

"Yes, certainly, I am Antonio Strollo," replied the latter.

"Do you know Antonio Torsielli?" continued Petrosini.

"To be sure," answered Strollo. "I knew him well," he added almost insolently.

"Why did you accompany him to New York?" inquired Petrosini sharply. Strollo paled. He had not known that the police were aware of the fact.

"I had errands in the city. I needed clothes," said Strollo.

"He has been murdered," said Petrosini quietly. "Will you come to New York to identify the body?"

Strollo hesitated.

"Why—yes—certainly. I will go to New York." Then he added, thinking that his words seemed insufficient, "I am sorry if Torsielli has been murdered, for he was a friend of mine."

There was a wait of several hours before the train started for New York and Strollo utilized it by giving Petrosini a detailed account of his trip with Torsielli. He took his time about it and thought each statement over very carefully before he made it, for he was a clever fellow, this Strollo. He even went into the family history of Torsielli and explained about the correspondence with the long-lost brother, in which he acted as amanuensis, for he had come to the conclusion that in the long run honesty (up to a certain point) would prove the best policy. Thus he told the detective many things which the latter did not know or even suspect. Strollo's account of what had happened was briefly as follows:

He and Toni had reached New York about twelve o'clock and had spent an hour or so in the neighborhood of Mott Street looking at the parade of "San Rocco." Then they had started for Yonkers and gone as far as the terminal of the Second Avenue El. It was about five o'clock in the afternoon. They had got out and started to walk. As they proceeded they suddenly had seen a man standing under a tree and Torsielli had said to Strollo:

"That man standing under that tree looks like my brother."

Strollo had replied:

"You know I am not acquainted with your brother."

As they reached the tree the stranger had stepped forward and said to Torsielli:

"Who are you?"

"Who? Me? My name is Antonio Torsielli," had been the reply. "Who are you?"

"I am Vito Torsielli," had answered the stranger. Then the two had rushed into each other's arms.

"And what did *you* do?" inquired Petrosini, as Strollo naïvely concluded this extraordinary story.

"Me?" answered Strollo innocently. "Why, there was nothing for me to do, so I went back to New York."

Petrosini said nothing, but bided his time. He had now several important bits of evidence. By Strollo's own account he had been with the deceased in the general locality of the murder shortly before it occurred; he had given no adequate explanation of why he was in New York at all; and he was now fabricating a preposterous falsehood to show that he had left his victim before the homicide was committed. On the train Petrosini began to tie up some of the loose ends. He noticed the wound on Strollo's hand and asked where it had been obtained. The suspect replied that he had received it at the hands of a drunken man in Mott Street. He even admitted having stayed at the Mills Hotel the same evening under an assumed name, and gave as an excuse that his own name was difficult for an American to pronounce and write. Later, this information led to the finding of the bloody bedclothes. He denied, however, having changed his clothes or purchased new ones, and this the detective was obliged to ferret out for himself, which he did by visiting or causing to be visited almost every Italian shop upon the East Side. Thus the incident of the shoes was brought to light.

Strollo was at once taken to the morgue on reaching the city, and here for the first time his nerve failed him, for he could not bring himself to inspect the ghastly body of his victim.

"Look," cried Petrosini; "is that the man?"

"Yes, yes," answered the murderer, trembling like a leaf. "That is he."

"You are not looking at him," said the detective. "Why don't you look at him. Look at the body."

"I *am* looking at him," replied Strollo, averting his eyes. "That is he—my friend—Antonio Torsielli."

The prisoner was now taken to Police Headquarters and searched. Here a letter was found in his hip pocket in his own handwriting purporting to be from Antonio Torsielli to his brother Vito at Yonkers, but enclosed *in an envelope addressed to Antonio at Lambertville.*

This envelope bore a red two-cent stamp and was inscribed:

ANTONIO   TORSIELLI,   BOX   470,
        Lambertville, New Jersey.

The letter as later translated in court by the interpreter read as follows:

LAMBERTVILLE, *July 30, 1905.*
My dear Brother:

Upon receipt of your news I feel very happy to feel you are well, and the same I can assure you from me. Dear Brother, you cannot believe the joy I feel after such a long time to know where you are. I have been looking for you for two years, and never had any news from you. I could not, as you wrote to me to, come to you, because I had no money, and then I didn't know where to go because I have been always in the country. Know that what little money I have I sent it to mother, because if I don't help her nobody will, as you never write to her. I believe not to abandon her, because she is our mother, and we don't want her cursed. So then, if you like to see me, you come and take me. You spoke to me about work thither, but I don't understand about that work which you say, and then what will I do because here I have work, therefore, if you think I can come and work with you let me know because I have the address. But if you want to do better you come and take me. *Dear Brother,* I remind you about our mother, because I don't earn enough money, which she is your mother also. DEAR BROTHER, I hope you did not forget our mother. Dear Brother, let me know the names of your children, and I kiss them. Many regards to your wife and Aunt. I beg you to write to me. Dear regards, your brother, Antonio Torsielli. When you answer send the answer to the address below, Antonio Strollo.

Strollo made no attempt to explain the possession of this letter, which, if sent at all would naturally have come into the possession of the addressee.

"And what was Vito's address at Yonkers?" inquired Petrosini.

"1570 Yonkers," answered Strollo.

"Is that the street number of a house or a post-office number?" asked the detective.

"Neither," said Strollo. "Just 1570 Yonkers."

Thus the infamy of this villain was made manifest. He had invented out of his own brain the existence of Vito Torsielli in Yonkers, and had himself written the letters to Antonio which purported to come from him. He had used the simple fellow's love for his long-lost brother as the means to lure him to his destruction, and brutally murdered him for the sake of the few dollars which his innocent victim had worked so hard to earn to reunite him to his mother and his betrothed.

The wounds in Strollo's hand and knee were found to correspond in shape and character with the thirty-six wounds in Torsielli's body, and the mushroom digger unhesitatingly identified him as the man in the company of the deceased upon the afternoon of the murder.

It almost seemed like the finger of Providence indicating the assassin when the last necessary piece of evidence in this extraordinary case was discovered. Petrosini had hurried to Lambertville immediately upon the discovery of the letter and visited the post-office.

A young lady named Miss Olive Phillips had been employed there as a clerk for twelve years, and had lately had charge of what are known as the "call boxes"—that is to say, of boxes to which no keys are issued, but for the contents of which the lessees have to ask at the delivery window. These are very inexpensive and in use generally by the Italian population of Lambertville, who are accustomed to rent them in common—one box to three or four families. She had noticed Strollo when he had come for his mail on account of his flashy dress and debonair demeanor. Strollo's box, she said, was No. 420. Petrosini showed her the envelope of the letter found in Strollo's pocket. The stamp indicated that it had been cancelled at *Lambertville* on July 26. When she saw the envelope she called Petrosini's attention to the fact that the stamp was a two-cent red stamp, and said, to his surprise, that she was able to identify the letter on that account as one *mailed* by *Strollo* on July 26. As there is no local delivery in the town, she explained, "drop letters," or letters mailed by residents to other residents, may be franked for one cent. Now, in the first place, no Italian in Lambertville, except Strollo, so far as Miss Phillips could remember, had ever mailed a letter to another Italian in the same town. A frugal Italian, moreover, if he had done so, would have put on only the required amount of postage. On the 26th of July, Strollo had come to the post-office and pushed this identical letter through the window, at the same time handing her two cents and asking her to put on a red stamp for him. She had been surprised at this, and had at first thought of calling his attention to the fact that only a one-cent stamp was necessary, but she had refrained and put on the stamp. At the same time she had noticed that it was addressed to "Antonio Torsielli, Lambertville, New Jersey." Strollo had then taken the letter and slipped it into the "drop" and she had cancelled the stamp, taking the opportunity to examine the letter a second time. A stranger coincidence could hardly be imagined, and this observing young lady from the country was thus able to supply the most important link in the chain against the murderer, and to demonstrate conclusively that the wretch had himself been mailing in Lambertville the letters purporting to come from the fictitious brother in Yonkers.

Strollo was now placed in the House of Detention as a "witness," a course frequently pursued when it is desirable to prevent a suspect from knowing that he is accused.

The case against him was practically complete, for it did not seem humanly possible, that any jury would hesitate to convict him upon the evidence, but juries are loath to find any one guilty of murder in the first degree upon purely circumstantial evidence, and this was the first purely circumstantial case in a long time. Inspector Price, therefore, conceived the idea of trapping Strollo into a confession by placing a detective in confinement with him under the guise of being a fellow-prisoner. It was, of course, patent that Strollo was but a child mentally, but he was shrewd and sly, and if he denied his guilt, there was still a chance of his escape. Accordingly, a detective named Repetto was assigned to the disagreeable task of taking the part of an accused criminal. He was detailed to the House of Detention and remained there for five days, from September 8 to September 13. Here Repetto became acquainted with Strollo and the other prisoners, giving his name as Silvio del Sordo and his address as 272 Bowery. He played cards with them, read the papers aloud and made himself generally agreeable. During this period he frequently saw the defendant write and familiarized himself with his chirography.

The scheme worked and Repetto afterward received five letters from Strollo, sent after the latter had been removed from the House of Detention to the Tombs and indicted for the murder of Torsielli. The first, dated September 22d, was merely to inform his supposed friend Silvio of the change in his residence and to inquire the whereabouts of another prisoner named Philip. The second would be pathetic were it not written by the defendant in the case. It carries with it the flavor of the Calabrian hills.

NEW YORK, *October 17, 1905.*

SIR SILVIO:

I write and believe not to sicken you with my words, but it is enough that you are well in health. I take the liberty again not having any one else but you, and I believe to find a brother in you, not a friend. I ask you nothing, only if you have time to come and see me as soon as possible. I ask you this as a favor because I know and believe to find a true friend, as I want to ask you a certain thing at the cost of my life. I will not say any more. Bring me five cents of paper and envelopes to write letters and when you come I will give you the money. Nothing else. I am yours ever. Servant and

Perfect friend,

A STROLLO.

The third letter from the perfect friend to his equally perfect friend is an extraordinary combination of ingenuity and ignorance. It contains the only suggestion of a defence—that of an alibi.

NEW YORK, *October 30, 1905.*

ESTEEMED FRIEND:

With retard I answer in receiving yours. I was very, very glad. I believe all you told me and I am grateful, and hope you will not betray me, because you know it will cost the life of a poor unfortunate, so do as you told me, keep things to ourselves, if you wish to help me you will do me a great service, and if God helps me, you can dispose of my life.

So I will have you called unexpected, saying that I did not know if you remembered. So if you are called the first thing you must do is to make believe to look at me, and then you say you remember of having seen me looking at the pictures in front of place where you work, and you asked me if I wanted my pictures taken and I said no. If they ask at what time say 5:20 or 5:30 P.M., and that you spoke with me for quite awhile. If they ask how was he dressed? The coat was black, the shoes russet the Trousers with white stripes which is the one I am now wearing; what tie, I don't remember, I only know he was well dressed, the hat was brown, if they ask did he have a mark on his hand? Say no, he had a ring with a black stone, how many times did you see him, say that after your work you were going around Mott Street and you saw me again and how it was eight o'clock or past eight and you saw me with a handkerchief around my hand, and you said to me, why I had my hand so. And he answered that some one struck him, I asked if it hurt much, he said he did not feel it, did both of you go to drink. No. Where else did Strollo go, Strollo said he was going at the Bleecker Street Hotel to sleep, did you see him again. No. Nothing else, if you want to help me reflect well, but you don't need any more words from me say just what I have said and I hope, with faith of a brother not a friend, I am ever your Friend,

A. STROLLO.

It may, and probably will, appear to the reader that a clearer case of guilt could hardly be established, but the action of juries is always problematical, and this was a case composed entirely of circumstantial evidence. The jury would be obliged to find that no reasonable hypothesis consistent with the innocence of the accused could be formulated upon the evidence. Thus, even in the face of the facts proven against him, some "freak" juryman might still have said, "But, after all, how do you *know* that Strollo killed him? Some *other* fellow might have done it." Even the "faking" of a defence does not prove the defendant guilty, but merely that he fears conviction, and is ready to resort to feigned testimony to secure his freedom. Many innocent men convict themselves in precisely this way.

Accordingly it was by no means with confidence that the People went to trial, but throughout this remarkable case it seemed as if it must have been preordained that Strollo should not escape punishment for his treacherous crime. No defence was possible, not even the partially prepared alibi was attempted, and the only thing that savored of a defence was the introduction of a letter alleged to have been received by the defendant while in the House of Detention, and which, if genuine, would have apparently established that the crime had been perpetrated by the "Black Hand."

The offering of this letter was a curious and fatal blunder, for it was later proven by the People to be in Strollo's own handwriting. It was his last despairing effort to escape the consequences of his crime. Headed with a cross drawn in blood it ran as follows:

I swear upon this cross, which is the blood of my veins, Strollo is innocent. I swear upon the cross the revengeful Black Hand could save me. New York, Oct. 12, 1905. Sir Strollo, knowing you only by name, eight days after that I leave this letter will be sent to you. I leave at seven o'clock with the Steamer Britain the Harbor. Therefore I leave betraying my oath that I have held for the last three years belonging to the Black Hand. I will leave three letters, one to you, one to the Police Officer Capri, and the other to the law, 300 Mulberry Street. All what I am saying I have sworn to before God. Therefore your innocence will be given you, first by God and then by the law, capturing the true murders. I am sure that they already captured the murderer of Torsielli. Who lured you to come to New York was Giuseppi Rosa, who knew you for nearly two years, and who comes from Lambertville, came among us and played you a trick. He is a Calabrise and has a mighty grudge. He and four others are averse to them. Announce the name of the man who stabbed you with the knife was Antonio Villa. He had to kill *you*, but *you* was fortunate. He is in jail for the present time and I don't know for how long, but I know that he was arrested. Nothing else to say. I have done my duty in giving you all the information. 407 2nd St., Jersey.

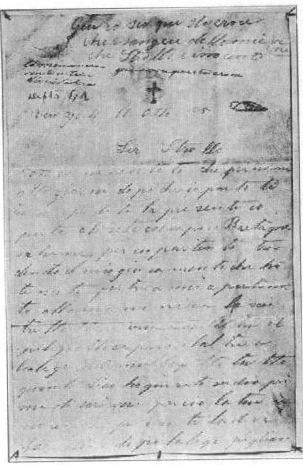

First page of the "Black Hand" letter written by Strollo, and put in evidence at his trial, placing the murder of Torsielli upon members of that imaginary secret organization. This letter convicted him.

It is clear from the letter that Strollo had formed a vague plan for his defence, which should, in part, consist of the claim that he, as well as Torsielli, had been marked for death by the Black Hand, and that while both had been induced to come to New York, the plans of the assassins had in his case miscarried.

The reader has already observed that purely for the purpose of securing his continued interest in the present narrative the writer has, as it were, told his story backward, reserving as long as possible the fact that the finding of the beloved Vito was a pure fiction invented by the murderer. At the trial, however, the jury listened breathlessly while bit by bit the whole pathetic story was painted before them, like a mosaic picture. They heard first the story of the mushroom digger, there of the expedition of Petrosini to Lambertville, of the identification of Torsielli's body, of the elaborate fabrications of Strollo, and in due course, of the tell-tale letter in the murderer's pocket. Gradually the true character of the defendant's crime came over them and they turned from him in aversion. The natural climax in the evidence was Miss Phillip's extraordinary identification of the defendant sitting at the bar as the man who had mailed upon the 26th of July, at the Lambertville post-office, the envelope purporting to come from Yonkers and containing the forged letter from the imaginary Vito.

Strollo remained almost to the last confident that he could never be convicted, but when his own letters in prison were introduced in evidence he turned ashen pale and stared fixedly at the judge. The jury deliberated but fifteen minutes, their functions consisting of but a single ballot, followed by a prayer for the wretched murderer's soul. Then they filed slowly back and, in the waning light of the summer afternoon just one year after the murder, and at the precise hour at which Strollo had killed his victim, pronounced him guilty of murder in the first degree. In due course his conviction was sustained by the Court of Appeals, and on March 11th, 1908, he paid the penalty for his crime in the electric chair.

Made in the USA
San Bernardino, CA
13 February 2020

64434800R00082